Tjernquist Förlag has published:
Stockholm Öarnas Stad   1982
Stockholm City of Islands 1983
Sverige — Ett Land i Norr   1984

Sweden—Land of the North is produced by Stig Tjernquist Annonsbyrå AB.
Stig Tjernquist has functioned as Art Director, in collaboration with Liz Elfgren and
Anette Tjernquist. Liz Elfgren and Anette Tjernquist selected the pictures, and are
responsible for the graphic design. The photo agencies of Bildhuset, Naturfoto-
graferna and TioFoto have provided pictures taken by 32 different photographers.
The legally responsible editer is Taisto Jalamo. 28 different writers have lent their
personal character to the respective chapters. The Swedish text has been translated
by Keith Bradfield, for Exportspråkgruppen. The proofs have been read by Lars
Roselius. The text has been composed by Sätteriet A & O AB, the headings in Futura
Bold, the bulk of the text in Frutiger Light. Lithography by KåPe-Grafiska. Printers:
Stellan Ståls Tryckerier. This book is printed on 170 g Macoprint. Bookbinding by
Barresjö Bokbinderi AB.

SWEDEN -
LAND OF THE NORTH

TJERNQUIST

CONTENTS

TO MAUD A.

AND MY FRIENDS: ANETTE T. BERRA C. BOSSE A. BOSSE (P) J. DICKE W. LEIF P. LINE C. LIZ E. PAJAS von K. PERCY K. PETER T. and SONJA N.

PREFACE

Travelling the huge length and less considerable breadth of our highly varied countryside, the idea has often occurred to me of recording the views and feelings that strike you as you travel, province by province, through Sweden. Each province, indeed each county, has its particular and subtle character, and the terrain constantly shifts in new and exciting ways.

The illustrations in this book have been provided by some 30 of Sweden's best nature photographers. They have captured their favourite areas with evident depth of feeling, and invite us to a splendid tour through Sweden.

To clarify further the specific character of Sweden's various provinces, I have asked a number of writers, known and less well-known, with close associations to their various regions, to write, simply, from their hearts. The texts they have produced constitute a broad assortment indeed, from historical and natural descriptions to fairytales and short stories.

A picture, they say, says more than a thousand words, but I do feel that in this book the written word clarifies most excellently the picture given of each province.

With which, let me wish you a pleasant trip through Sweden!

Stig Tjernquist

SKÅNE

Skania—a visual suite
Here the sun shines like a poppy
over meadowlands
and the bright rape's yellow flowers
blind the villagers.
You can see for miles around
the well-kept farm estates
dozing sleepily,
in quiet affluence.

Round castles and round manors
swans swim gracefully
(the nobility have survived here,
and the windmills too).

Past Skanör and Falsterbo
see the birds migrating.
In Helsingborg and Malmö
hear the ferries hooting.
Over Lund's impressive Minster
History's wings are beating,
whispering of the day
when this, the Danes' archbishopric,
was strongest in the North.

While the fair-haired local maiden
Curved like the Earth our Mother
Loves softly and enjoyingly
Just as she's always done
Her Skanian—and none other.
by Bernt Staf

Österlen—south-eastern Skåne

In howling storms, or through sun-bright waters, the fishing boats return to Simrishamn, the largest fishing port in Sweden. If the weather has been good, they will for the most part have 200—400 boxes of ice-packed fish on board. Then the mood will be lively; celebrations, girl-friends and wives await them. The anxiety looses its grip on the small fishing villages. This is a dangerous job.

But bad weather seldom gives any catches. Then the men lie, at best, in their bunks. The boat groans and plunges down into the waves; the diesel roars and gets out of breath, as the propeller churns the air to pieces before the stern falls again, and the men are pressed for an instant against their bunks. The next moment they are weightless. The stench of diesel oil and rotting fish remains, pursuing them into their dreams and hallucinations as they are tossed to and fro, to and fro, by the turbulent sea.

The Österlen coast has rich traditions in shipping.

When Skåne became Swedish in 1658, it was only natural that trade should run via eastern Skåne, since the eastern side was closer to Sweden-Finland and the Baltic provinces, while its west coast was under constant threat from the bitter Danes, who regarded Skåne as more genuinely Danish than their vassal state of Norway.

The Österlen fleet's period of greatness coincided with the closing era of the sailing ships, which is to say the turn of the century. Along 18 miles or so of coastline, from Kivik in the north to Skillinge in the south, were at most some 300 merchant ships, which sailed the world over. Brantevik was the home port of Sweden's largest single fleet of sailing ships, which included, at most, 118 merchantmen.

To the visitor from outside, Österlen today appears as a well-groomed, park-like, slumbering idyll. The villages lie at a distance of some 3—4 km from each other, with a 12th century church in the middle, and, around the village, the sugar beet, corn, and brilliant yellow rape, often with great red streaks of poppy. Sometimes the poppies shine so magnificently that the fields look like the flag of Skåne, a yellow cross on a red field.

The chiaroscuro of the beech forests, with their pillared halls; the long white sandy beaches; the exotic flora at Stenshuvud; the passageway graves, rock carvings, and royal burial mounds throughout the billowing province; the stormlashed enchanted forest at Sandhammaren; the stones of Ale; the palaces, the great houses, the old inns, the rush roofs and half-timbering: all this suggests an abandoned paradise.

Because the farmer these days works in technological solitude. Bumping along in his tractor, pop music spouting from his freestyle ear protectors if he is young, wearing a gas mask when he mixes and sprays his poisons.

Is it possible that the rationalisation of industry, and of our office landscapes, will lead to fewer poisonous substances and more human beings being employed in environment management, forestry, and farming?

Österlen dreams, and bides its time.
by Bernt Staf

BLEKINGE

To make your way through the countryside by bicycle, along the many back roads, produces something of a jigsaw feeling. Suddenly, you find yourself ringed in by the timeless nooks and crannies of rural life, by remote villages that have hidden behind hazel-covered slopes, and entwined themselves in whole thickets of flowers. It's as if you were approaching the very bedchamber of the Sleeping Beauty. In that case, let her sleep on. The great blustering Time outside afforded you no happiness, only emptiness, a garnished nothing, disappointment. Let no Prince come and wake her.

Harry Martinsson

HALLAND

A short tale of the coastal wind

In a house by the sea, three men sat talking. It was early one morning before all history, before the wind had made the coast people tight-lipped and permanently hunched.

Through the dark room rolled from time to time a blowing wave of violet — a reflection of sunsets. The men's talk grew louder, causing the flames of the fire to cast red gleams in the dark wine jugs on the table.

Suddenly, the three men burst into ringing laughter. The fire went out, and ash whirled into the room. They looked at each other in amazement, while their laughter rolled to and fro over the floor. They rose, standing bolt upright, and deep below them their chairs slipped away like shadows.

"I'll go out first," said the youngest, brushing the ash from the corner of his eyes. He opened the door, gave a whistle — and was wafted slowly away over the violet hog-backs of the coast.

It was beginning to get light.

The oldest man proceeded giggling to the door, which stood swinging in the blast. He closed it slowly behind him, and, leaning cautiously forward, sauntered towards the birch in whose crown the overcoat of the first man to leave could be glimpsed. Above it, in the hazy sky, ran soles of feet, faint tracks slowly fading in the wind.

The man saw this, and shouted. The gale filled his lungs, and he rose with the wind and clouds obliquely to the northeast.

With his lips tightly closed, and his toes curled, the third man set off across the yard in front of the house, which sloped down towards the sea. Pondering the fate of his two friends, he made his way along the shore, lashed by the wind, leaning away from the gale-swept sea, in towards the land.

He clenched his teeth tightly together — biting his lip in the process. His howl of pain chased away all the gulls, but the gale swept into his wide-open mouth. And he too was raised by the wind and raging weather to the passing clouds.

by Alf Hambe

SMÅLAND

What is Småland?

"Småland", you say, "is the largest province in Götaland, with an area of 31,698.45 sq. km.; it comprises the counties of Jönköping, Kronoberg and Kalmar, with the exception of Öland. The bedrock of the Småland highlands consists essentially of primary rock, in the southwestern half shale-bearing iron gneiss, and in the eastern half granites, with elements of hard porphyries and leptites. The forests, once the poor man's overcoat and the Smålander's farmland, cover over half the surface of Jönköping and Kronoberg Counties, and more than a third that of Kalmar County. Småland is one of the Swedish provinces most rich in lakes, and Kronoberg County has more lakes than any other. Jönköping and Kronoberg counties are among those most characterized by small-scale farming; industry, particularly small-scale industry, is also important. You must have heard of the 'Gnosjö spirit'?".

"Yes," I answer. "but Småland is not just a piece of physical reality, unambiguous, and the same to everyone. Småland is also the images we carry in our hearts, each with its own colour, form, and shimmer upon the world. Småland is always *someone's* Småland, and accordingly it changes, from one person to another.

"I remember the Swedish American, employed at the Pentagon, and with the rank of a two-star general, whom I and my wife Gudrun drove through the countryside of Småland in our little Daf. He was astounded by all the well-kept farms, painted in Falu red, that we passed, bearing, each of them, their rose-coloured testimony to well-being; he saw in amazement the broad, asphalted roads, with their sparse traffic, laid down through the Småland forests. He recalled the gaunter Småland of his childhood, with its narrow, winding gravel roads, the lilacs blooming around the cottages, the eternal labour of cleaning the small vegetable plots from their stones, and the poverty that hovered so constantly at people's doors. For him, the images he took to his heart were those of an unimagined well-being, an unexpected welfare, a wealth that he had not envisaged in the 'old country' which he had not visited for 50 years". "And your picture of Småland", you ask, "what's that?"

"My picture", I answer, "is one of a grassy sward, studded with white wood anemones, in early May, surrounding an old schoolhouse in Lönneberga, perched on the edge of the Småland highlands. On three sides, the forest stands dense and high, apparently full of life and vigour, but here as elsewhere threatened by the Tree Death that is insinuating itself through the dark shadows of the firs. The building stands in a sparsely populated area, and you don't have to travel far afield to encounter the poor relics of abandoned villages, which reveal the rapid transformation the farmlands of Småland are undergoing." But whatever the images we carry in our hearts, they all represent a world that needs our care and friendship if it is to survive, and we with it. Once, Man fought against Nature; now we need another approach to her, in harmony and inwardness, with respect for the uniqueness of all things. Perhaps we have come to understand, at last, that our own nature, human nature, is but an extension of the wild kingdom within us."

by Sandro Key Åberg

ÖLAND

The ghosts of Öland

For ages, he had been dying for some peace and quiet. The crowds and traffic of the capital had got on his nerves. He was tired of the eternal drunken murmur of the pubs, and the never-ending talk of his friends about women, and about the books they one day intended to write. So he was highly delighted when the opportunity arose to borrow a little cottage on Öland, in the heart of the Alvaret heathlands. Autumn was already drawing in, but he cheerfully packed his rucksack and set off for this low-lying island off the east coast of Sweden.

At that time, Öland was not yet linked by bridge to the mainland, and he had to take the ferry between Kalmar and Färjestaden. Öland had a sense of isolation about it, it was a world of its own. Indeed, he felt, it was as if he had been transported back to another age. To the Viking Age, or still further back in the dim past.

Broken-winged windmills lined his route as he hiked from the bus-stop in the falling dusk in towards the centre of the island. There was not a human being in sight, only low-flying magpies flapping across Alvaret like wet dishcloths. He began to feel uncomfortable. There was something eerie about this swampy countryside, in which no life was discernible, and the only sound to be heard, apart from the scornful laughter of the magpies, was that of his own footsteps on the narrow, winding, gravel path.

He had no difficulty in finding the cottage, since it was the only building in the place. Or, more accurately, the only building that still had a roof and windows intact. Of what had once been a prosperous village, there remained only rows of dilapidated, rotting wooden buildings. Here and there, ragged shutters on broken hinges beat upon decaying grey walls. Gnarled trees stretched out their arms to embrace him. The cottage was almost overgrown with scrubby bushes and grass the height of a man.

With some difficulty, he managed to open the door to the conservatory, which was jam-packed with rusty bicycles. Apart from the conservatory, the cottage consisted of a large room with an open, whitewashed fireplace and a little kitchen, in which a stove on cast-iron feet crouched in the corner like an evil monster, covered in cobwebs. He made haste to light a fire, before darkness overcame the cottage entirely. Smoke blew in from the fireplace, and the light of the paraffin lamp was hardly enough for him to make the necessary preparations for his supper. The wind tore at the roof tiles, as he heated his food from the tin.

"Betake yourself to Helgafjäll, and go up to the loft above the outer door. There, remove some planks in the floor, so that you can stick a spear through the hole.

"When Snorre goes to the privy, set the spear through the loft floor and into Snorre's back with such force that it comes out through his stomach. Run then out onto the roof, descend by the wall, and let the darkness of night conceal you."

He sat by the fireside reading a book, sipping from time to time from his bottle of *brännvin.* Just as he sank for a while in contemplation of the flames, he heard a copper horn sounding out on the now moonlit heath. And he could hear the measured clash of sword upon shield ... Rigid with fright, he crept to the window and wiped the mist from the pane, peering out into the night. And there they came! Side by side, hefty, bearded men with helmets covering their faces so that only their eyes gleamed in the black holes. Heavy round shields and huge broadswords reflected the moonlight, as the berserks relentlessly approached over the heath ...

He fell, time and again, from his rusty bicycle as he peddled for dear life through the moonlit Öland night, the bare rims of his wheels rattling infernally in the gravel ...

Every time his friends at the pub subsequently raised matters literary for discussion, he would mutter that reading was the curse of mankind. But all this, as I have said, was before the Öland Bridge was built. Today, there's hardly a free space left on the island for ghosts and spirits. The tourists are swarming over Alveret like the locusts of Egypt ... Or maybe not?

by Taisto Jalamo

GOTLAND

Island in the sea

My heart is an island with a strange and changing pulse.

It was born in the sea. Its history began many hundreds of million years ago, with a sea lily that calcified. And when the island finally emerged, it was a limestone rock formed of coral, brachiopods, trilobites, and sea lilies.

It is this petrified world from a tropical sea that is the island of Gotland.

In March, the island is grey as a pencil drawing. When the storms of late winter collect the sparse snow in drifts over the rocky terrain, no Arctic tundra could be meaner. Where the lark in summer, like a fluttering crotchet, cheerfully warbles, only the snowflakes now dance, thousands upon thousands of them. Everything is white and grey, and the stunted firs are glad they are no taller.

At this time the ewes give birth. On snow-free patches in the shelter of the woods lie the newborn lambs, under the inspection of the cheerless, chill, blue-grey sky.

Seven March storms have to be counted before the spring can be accepted as spring.

But when the hawthorn strews white confetti over the branches, and the dandelions grow everywhere, possible and impossible, then at last it is spring. Soon the hazel leaves will resemble mouse's ears, and Nature will start weaving her floral carpets.

The yellow stonecrop alternates with violet orchids, while the pink-mauve wild chive forms sharp stripes beside the yellow swathes of rockrose.

At the beginning of June, patches of clear blue can appear on the ground. This is the viper's bugloss, igniting its flowers in the ditches, on the rock faces, and along the pebble beaches. Quite soon, it is thinned out with the poppies and moon-daisies.

Lying stretched out in the grass and flowers, you can hear their scents talking.

Red voices, speaking of love. Blue words, which speak of the life you are living. Yellow words on the strength of emotions. The white flowers speak quietly in the mornings, and are inaudible towards evening. But their language is beautiful. The sound is there, if only you are capable of listening.

In the heat of July you should walk along the island's shores, the sand running between your toes; or among fossils that imprint themselves on the soles of tender feet.

Every day, the beach is washed by the constantly rolling sea. The rays of the sun are caught by silver-glancing bits of water-polished wood. Fragments of the forests, of ships, of human artefacts are collected in the treasure-house of the shores. On some of these shores, the sea, over many thousands of years, has chiselled out from the limestone rock the formations known as *rauks*. The hard remains, with which the water has been unable to cope. These stone statues can assume the most enchanting shapes.

If you think that grey is dull, then you may not like *rauk* country. But their grey contains a wealth of shades from the sunlight, rain, storm and snow.

To sit on the shore of the *rauks* and hear the sea talking to the gulls, and feel the warmth of the stones — this is to be a very small part of something great.

The autumn is a later summer.
cont'd page 37

The sea yields up the warmth it has gathered, and the evergreen tops of the stunted firs dampen the feeling of autumn. Only in the leafy meadows does the fire of colours rage, and in occasional patches along the fringes of the forest.

The wind is almost always there, as a breeze, or as a raging storm. The warm zephyrs of summer are as fair as October's savage gales are frightening. Then, practically the whole of Visby is drenched as the sea wrestles the shore, and the mediaeval packing-houses and ring wall are painted dark grey by the foam.

Around the coasts, the sea also acts as gardener. The trees, incapable of growing upwards, follow the ground like crawling creatures. Their roots and branches, blending with their trunks, form ornamental patterns beneath their leafy crowns.

Storms are both seen and heard on this flat island.

Heavy, indigo-blue clouds roll over the landscape, the thunder knocks at people's doors as if wanting to come in.

But when the worst of the rain has passed, the storm gods can draw the most astonishing rainbows, with both ends visible. Seldom are these spectral bridges of raindrops seen so in their entirety as here.

This is also an island of mists.

In the autumn and spring, when the fog and mist rise from the sea to draw their grey blankets over the terrain, everything vanishes into obscurity.

The houses on Gotland are perhaps part of nature to a higher degree than in other provinces.

Built of the same stone as the island itself, piled by hand, or of resinous trunks of pine, laid as a bulwark.

Raised high, with slate roofs, or lower buildings with roofs of hoary planking. The stone houses of Gotland grow to a ripe old age.

But some of them do die, from lack of maintenance. And seldom do you see an edifice decaying with such elegance as an unmortared stone house.

To the end of its days, it rises up to the skies. Its empty windows are eyes, looking out over their landscape. All its naked stones are grey, the grey of old age, with a tale to tell of people and events.

Until the last stone falls...

by Bo Forsberg

GÖTEBORG

All the way down from the north
"You're going to Gothenburg", they told me in a tone demanding that I look pleased. YOU ARE GOING, they meant, AWAY. One thousand three hundred kilometres south to a big city, away from your little home in the bay, your father, and your Lapp dog. I was eleven years old, and wanted to stay at home.

My strongest feeling as the train drew into Gothenburg was watchfulness. A watchfulness that sharpened to bitter criticism when I saw through the taxi window the ugly great buildings of yellow-brown brick. The woman who met me had food ready and waiting at home, a special West Coast fish with green bones, boiled, and served to my complete incomprehension with chive sauce. After struggling for some min- utes to distinguish between the fish bones and chives, I burst into tears of desperate disappointment. "I want to go home to my dad!" I sobbed.

After a good night's sleep, my pes- simism had given way to curiosity. I caught sight of a black silk kimono, with gold print: beautiful or exotic things have always excited in me a feverish desire. The question was, how could I grab it? The issue was resolved only when we left the flat, moving out to an Lotment-garden cottage by Slottskogen. What a fantastic forest, I thought, gazing reverently out upon oak, beech, poplar, and willow. Back in Norrland, the deciduous trees had been birch, rowen, alder and aspen.

In the evenings, ugly complaining sounds were to be heard from the woods. Peacocks, they told me. Peacocks I had only seen painted on my grandmother's best china, and I refused to believe that these magnificent birds produced sounds worse than the gulls.

The bright summer nights of Norr- land were replaced by darkness, and I had to contend with constant false in- structions from my own time machine.

They took me to a packed bathing beach. Having grown up with a sandy cove to myself, I was dumbfounded. I saw a boy with freckles, dark and large as peppercorns. Italian, they said. Since I got a few freckles of my own every spring, I at least did not draw the chil- dish conclusion that all Italians were freckled. But I stored his alien appear- ance in my memory. In retrospect, I can swear that he looked above all Jewish.

There were some indescribably beautiful starfish in the water, but hor- rid, scuttling crabs frightened me back to land.

The children in the area were a bit older, and their attitude to me was more than somewhat rudimentary. And I felt ridiculous; children from the coun- try always feel that they are comical to city children.

A trip in the archipelago was an event in itself. And at one point the little steamer stopped, and everyone looked in the same direction. The only Swedish submarine to have been sunk during the war had just been salvaged, with its dead crew. The submarine "Owl". An historic, or at least dramatic, sight.

Little did I know then, that wherever I went my life would consist of just this — one drama after another.

by Loka Enmark

40

BOHUSLÄN

Of all Sweden's varied landscapes, that of Bohuslän draws most clearly and strictly the boundary between language and the world. You don't have to search particularly long for the word that best communicates one's sense of inadequacy when faced with its terrain: Nature here is manifestly *intractable*.

Language is abstraction. The Bohuslän countryside is an abstraction of Nature, the world reduced to a few constituent parts, dumb and internal signs. As I try to describe the landscape, I describe it with my feelings when confronted by it. I try to translate what I see into language; translating from the one enclosed system of signs to another.

My ineffectiveness, this impotence of both reason and emotion, is as close to love as makes no difference. If I describe the woman I love, I speak about her in analogies. And in the case of Nature, which man can exploit but never understand since he is part of her, the analogies become still more adventurous, extended, strained.

There are landscapes so rich in colour, movement and shape as to lend themselves easily to the observer as living mirrors. There are landscapes in which the play of lines, fragrances and sounds is so lively, or so magnificent, as to excite admiration rather than respect, delight rather than sorrow.

But Bohuslän diminishes, rejects, refuses all words, emotions, thoughts.

If the forests of Värmland, the fells of Lappland, tell Man that he is small, then these muscular islands, these rocks of blood granite, the tossing glass-green sea, the damp, thrusting odours of seaweed and sedge, tell him he is nothing, that he does not exist.

Nature is the face of God. So it is hardly strange if people's religion in these parts is dark, severe and hard. Extravagance, sensual display and vanity are the signs not only of a sinful character, but of stupidity.

If you embellish, adorn, and paint, if you speak loudly and long—then you have to be stupid, deaf and blind to the violent stillness of the abrupt, rugged cliff-face as it plunges down into the acid, breathless water.

And when summer arrives, to the ragged bay a few miles north of Fjällbacka, then you must know that its shimmering blue smile is not addressed to us—it is the sky and the sea that are eyeing each other, embracing each other.

cont'd page 46

This is an early part of the world. A few plants, a few animals, and a single sort of human being have succeeded in clutching fast to this moment, to this thin membrane of humus and light that has been painted over the silent, grey and crimson-streaked granite.

Far away, along the bright red, millimetre-thin main road down there, the last bus comes into town. It is smaller than the ladybird on the blade of grass between those rocks. And 40 such as I will find room for in that bus. On this fact I chew, as on a dew-wet leaf of oyster plant.

On this fact, and on the word "intractable", an opal-sparkling abstraction that approaches the true form of the landscape; but at the last moment the landscape withdraws, as if to reject all language.

by Ragnar Strömberg

DALSLAND

Border country—and fairyland

In the forests along the border between Dalsland and Norway, you sometimes don't know what country you're in. The roads and paths are ancient. Here Charles XII passed through on his last, unfortunate campaign down to Halden, only to be shot in the head.

And the people speak Norwegian, on both sides of the frontier. Norwegians lease the Swedish farmland at Stora Le. They drive across with their machines in the morning, and back over the border at night: for many years, Sweden had a peculiar regulation that no Norwegian tools should be left in this country overnight.

In the old days, the Swedes used to drive over and shop in Norway, where everything was cheaper. Now it is only the Norwegian flour and margarine that are worth buying. Also, according to the children, they have better ice-cream.

The Norwegians drive nowadays down to the Swedish country store at Stora Le, to buy petrol and tobacco. The Swedish forests are owned by the Norwegian Sawmill Association down in Halden. Norwegian timber trucks thunder along the forest roads in Dalsland.

This is a wonderful landscape. The farm estates have been owned by the same families for centuries, and everyone is related to each other.

A hundred years ago, many Swedes emigrated to America, and Dalsland was one of the provinces that lost most people. Many never wrote home. But the children of many such emigrants now sail along the Dalsland Canal during the summers, and subscribe to the newspaper "Dalslänningen".

There are masses of Germans in the forests, picking lingonberries and mushrooms. The Germans' favourite Swedish provinces are Dalsland and Värmland, probably because there is still so much wild country here. They rent crofts deep in the forest, to which no roads lead.

This is a fairyland, filled with witchcraft. We met a man here who was slightly worried that he only had daughters, I can't remember how many. He went to a wise woman, who advised him to place an axe under the bed if he wanted a son.

He took his motor saw instead, and put it under the double bed. And lo and behold! His wife bore him twins, two boys.

This is a true story, but one that gains in the telling: many people hereabouts believe that you have to start up the motor saw before retiring!

by Lars Westman

VÄSTER-GÖTLAND

Rise up o'er the billowing barley,
Thou Midsummer Sun, shine now!
The crops all around filled, early,
The furrows of last year's plough;
Now rose-fingered dawn at its leisure
On the wheat paints a golden rain:
This sight in my heart will I treasure,
This view of our broad, rich plain.

The peasant's land is his money,
His wealth, which he'll ne'er forsake,
All flowing with milk and honey,
In his husbandry's busy wake.
His patience is sempiternal
And slow is he of reply,
But his words, like his wheat,
    have a kernel
And he'll never tell you a lie.

In cities, it may be the fashion
Less deeply to love, and to kiss:
The countryman's true in his passion
And faithful in wedded bliss.
There's children and youth here
    a-plenty
Of the ancient Teutonic blood,
To fill Sweden's veins, pale and empty,
With a nobler, more honest flood.

The farmhand was ta'en from his cattle
To fight mid the grim War's alarms
He rode for his King into battle
And returned with a coat of arms.
By the light of a candle, burning
The hind's son could his way seek
To the pleasant groves of learning,
And ascend Parnassus's peak.

In the days of the terrible hunger
When many the Reaper took
And the blessed rain fell no longer
And the country with terror shook,
The peasant, his courage unwaning
Made chaff-bread on which to dine,
And when that failed, still uncom-
    plaining
Used bark from the good red pine.

I know whence they drew the power
That caused them never to fail:
The church, with its proud white tower,
By the pastureland tells the tale:
The meekly bowed congregation,
The hymn that rises and swells,
In unending jubilation
To the sound of the holy bells.

Let foolish scholars keep turning
The pages of "history" they've penned;
For men can perhaps have learning,
Yet nothing of life comprehend.
The story of toil rewarded,
Of the splendid and golden plain
Is the one that should be recorded,
And sung of time and again.

Västergötarike, I hail thee
With the morning light all around:
Thy like let them seek, 'twill be vainly
Thy peer will never be found.
See there the farms' red lustre,
In the land where the cattle graze;
Like roses bright in a cluster,
In the lush fields they blaze.

Rise up o'er the billowing barley,
Thou Midsummer Sun shine now!
The crops all around filled, early,
The furrows of last year's plough:
So pour out your Horn of Plenty
Over Lake Vättern's strand
On this blessed place it empty—
God's peace upon Västgötaland!

by Paul Nilsson

The cranes
The cranes are coming! They're coming!

Someone's excited shout, and the rest of us stopped in our traces, petrified as tree-stumps, listening breathlessly, our mouths hanging half-open, for a sound in the air. And there it came! A crowing, trumpeting, cackling sound, high, high up under the grey bowl of heaven. Right enough, the cranes were coming, and we soon had the great avine plough in our glasses.

Majestically, with slow, casual wing-beats the flock proceeded straight as an arrow north-north-west towards the awaiting fenlands, the whole time with that loud, aggressive trumpeting. I was thirteen years old, a recently hatched field biologist, when I first saw and heard cranes, and I remember what a contradictory impression they made on me. On the one hand, this excited, ill-bred cackling; on the other, their ingratiating, courtly movements. A sort of mixture between noisy school playground and religious procession.
by Tommy Hammarström

ÖSTER-GÖTLAND

What is the soul of a province, or a region? The people who live there? The dialect? The countryside? Or is it perhaps both the people *and* the countryside, the countryside on which we all depend…

Perhaps the soul of a province lies in its lakes, its forests, its plains, and its coasts…

And nowadays, perhaps, in its industries and livelihoods, such as forestry and agriculture.

Östergötland is certainly a many-facetted province. With the enchanted forests of Kolmården, once so feared by travellers. With an archipelago that is still alive. And with its lakes. The severe shores and deep, clear waters of Lake Vättern. Sommen, with all its bays and islands, to the south. The classical Lake Tåkern, Sweden's most outstanding bird sanctuary. Roxen, Boren and Glan. Mirrors set in the landscape…

Or should we mention the rich, fertile plain, dating from time immemorial, which laid the foundation of Sweden's present welfare? If only it had not developed into a "monoculture" of wheat and rape!

To the west is the eternal silhouette of Omberg, a backdrop to the wide-open spaces. Omberg with its legendary tales, its Queen Omma, and its caves, hollowed out by the wild waters.

And below Omberg, the monastery of Alvastra, pitifully maltreated by Gustav Vasa who needed stone for his impressive castle at Vadstena. The monasteries in Skänningen, in their day an important Swedish "city", were similarly quarried; nowadays, Skänninge is known for its market, which attracts hundreds of thousands of visitors.

The souls of its saints and great men still hover, perhaps, over Östergötland: St. Brigit over Vadstena, Birger Jarl over Bjälbo, author Verner von Heidenstam over his Övralid, Baltzar von Platen over the length of his life's work, the Göta Canal, Bjare over his world-famous Smoke Stone, Urban Hjärne over salubrious Medevi Spa, and Bishop Brask over Linköping…

Or perhaps the soul of a province is to be sought within ourselves. Shaped by the countryside, by the people around us, and by our ability to embrace feelings, to experience, and to create.

by Christer Elderud

VÄRMLAND

The hunt by night

At midnight, just as the sun emerged from the clouds to illuminate the terrain with its pale blue light, the fox caught the scent of the hare. Red Fur was hungry, desperately hungry, and firmly determined to eat fresh, warm, bleeding meat this very night! With gleaming, intelligent, searching eyes, he slunk along the hollows and sloping banks of streams, approaching the hare with the help of shadows and cairns. Cunningly, he bided his time.

But although the hare's little three-cornered head was echoing like a mortar as he gnawed at the spring's first night-frosted shoots from the three-year-old pines, he instinctively discovered the danger with his long, constantly reconnaissing ears. The ears that were his only weapon, apart from his hind legs, in this cruel, demented world.

Like a ball of wool, the hare fled over the moonlit forest glades, to disappear the next instant under the shadows cast by heavy pines, and the next moment again rush out on some moonlit face of rock. Terror lent speed and vigour to his long hind legs, extending his bounds well beyond the hare's normal capacity. His speed was high, but eerily soundless; not a dry twig was broken, not a panting breath was to be heard in the resin-fragrant spring forest, where a few patches of grey-white snow still lingered between the cairns and beneath the dense, low-hanging branches of the pines. Death hunted the hare through the nocturnal forest; what he could not understand was how the fox could continue so obstinately and indefatigably, neither increasing nor reducing his speed, while the distance between them appeared to become constantly shorter. The slim, light-footed, soft-pawed hare had failed to comprehend the tactical error of running zig-zag. Every turn the prey made favoured Red Fur, under the principle of the shortest distance between two points being a straight line…

As clouds for an instant hid the moon, the hare took the opportunity to run into a clear-felled area, with a vague idea of being able to hide among the underbrush and bushes; but the fox never gave up, he was firm in his purpose. Hunger, and now also fury at this pathetic creature's refusal to provide his night's supper made him still more determined.

The hare was already aware that his strength was failing him, when he heard the sound of the river down in the valley; perhaps, the roar of the current would confuse his grim persecutor? He ran down towards the river.

Arriving safely at the river bank, the hare discovered that Red Fur could be neither seen nor heard. Relieved, he scuttled upstream along the brink of the river, and started looking for something to eat. His long ears pricked and searched, but could hear only the sound of the water, and the clatter of the rolling round stones that he set in motion with his soft, woolly paws.

Highest up on the river bank, at the edge of the forest, in the No man's land between shadow and moonlight, waited the fox, who had never abandoned his principle of the shortest distance between two points. Cunningly, he bided his time, observing his approaching steak… Briskly, Red Fur felled the hare and sank his jaws into its woolly throat. The hare's death cry echoed chillingly over the moonlit Värmland forests. *by Taisto Jalamo*

At Poetry's Gate
Humanity's Spirit at Poetry's Gate
Tells of her glorious deeds to date,
And all the brave deeds before her.
With this bright sun, beneath this sky:
Who'll give her the lie?
Who'll be unkind, or scorn her?
Though ill the tale become her.

The Spirit, she sits at Poetry's Gate
(Her constant state).
Magnificent eyebrows lifted high,
She surveys the sky;
Recalls how da Vinci began to write,
In Florence, about the swallow's flight;
At Benvenuto Cellini's, a feast;
And how Vasco da Gama set off for
    the East
(Remembering so well that day in May,
When they struck their sails in
    Calicut Bay).
So much, so much, both "nows"
    and "thens",
Image on image on eyeball's lens:
But what the effect, and what
    the cause?
What now "is" or "was"?
She knows of Moloch's pagan host,
And pyramids and altars,
And of much that wanders in
    darkness, lost
That whimpers, groans, and falters.

The Spirit, she sits at Poetry's Gate,
Of misty origin, unknown fate.
She's known the plague, and the
    trenches' mire
The whip, the fire
(Blood and evil attend her train
Through the cheering crowds, and the
    lonely pain).
But the dream, the vision, she
    carries still
Like bird-song over heath and hill,
A song that out of light is bred,
Over fountains sealed and houses
    dead.
Still all too gaudy our flags, unfurled
In what we call "God's wondrous
    world".
This, too, an aberration,
We claim as our salvation:
"All that's great beneath the sun
Or lights a fire,
This she has done."
She's counted the stars, their
    distance, pace
As they orbit steadily out in space.
She sits with her instruments and tools
The pilot of our ship of fools,
Herself of some lost wind a breath,
A birth-cry and a wrinkled death.
                    by Nils Ferlin

NÄRKE

In the case of Närke in particular, the geological perspective is a rewarding one. Even if it has its irritating aspects.

9 000–10 000 years ago, what is now Närke was the westernmost bay of Lake Ancylus, a lake considerably larger than the Baltic. In westernmost Närke ran the ridge of land that separated this lake from the Western (Atlantic) Ocean.

It was long believed that this lake ran into the sea at the "Svea Falls", just south of Degerfors. The body of water borne from the east was thought to have been three times that of Niagara, and the falls a full kilometre in breadth.

This picture has now proved more or less entirely false. There never were any "Svea Falls". The giant cauldrons and polished rock faces were produced when the River Svea (the River Let of our own day) came from the north, was trapped, and whirled around in various pockets of the mountains. A preferably-not-spoken of mishap in our older tourist brochures.

The northern shore of the great bay comprises now the hills of Kilsbergen, south of Tiveden and Hallsbergen. The rock appears to have cracked open at an angle of 25°, like gaping jaws with metal fillings, which have been prized open.

But not just any old fillings. These were the iron foundation of Sweden's era as a great power. The mining district of Lekeberg to the northwest, that of Lerbäck to the southeast. The latter rich not only in iron ore, but also in cobalt and zinc. The latter is now the only ore still mined in Närke.

On the bottom of this bay, now the Närke plains, under the protection of the hills, lies the Cambro-Silurian sandstone, with here and there patches of alum shale (which gave us Kvarntorpsindustrin, and met a great deal of our petrol and oil requirements during World War II).

The first settlement on the plain was established cautiously, with a great deal of languid trial and testing. By that time most of the great ice lake had drained off to the east, leaving numerous sounds behind it. "När" they were called in Old Swedish. "Rek" was the name given to the frontier area between the Svea and Västgöta peoples. And so they became "Närikar", the people who settled down on the hogbacks, driving down sticks for all their ingenious fish-traps (for bream), and scratching at their narrow plots of barley. But when they raised their eyes, they could see the blue contours of Kilsbergen. A slow, bog-dwelling people.

In the upper, forward part of the gaping old lake stands Örebro, a cement-fixated molar tooth at the western tip of Hjälmaren, the stony lake where a super abundance of crayfish died of disease at the beginning of this century, but where the pike-perch still run. And it is lined by two whole rows of castles and manor-houses.

Örebro and its castle stand at the tip of Svealand's water-glistening spear, whose handle is Stockholm. It is no wonder that, from the early 16th century when Bishop Hans Brask first put forward the idea, right up to cannon designer Carl Christian Engström's detailed drawings of 1910, great plans have always been entertained for a "Svea Canal" from the Baltic, through Närke, to the Kattegatt.

by Peter Eckerbom

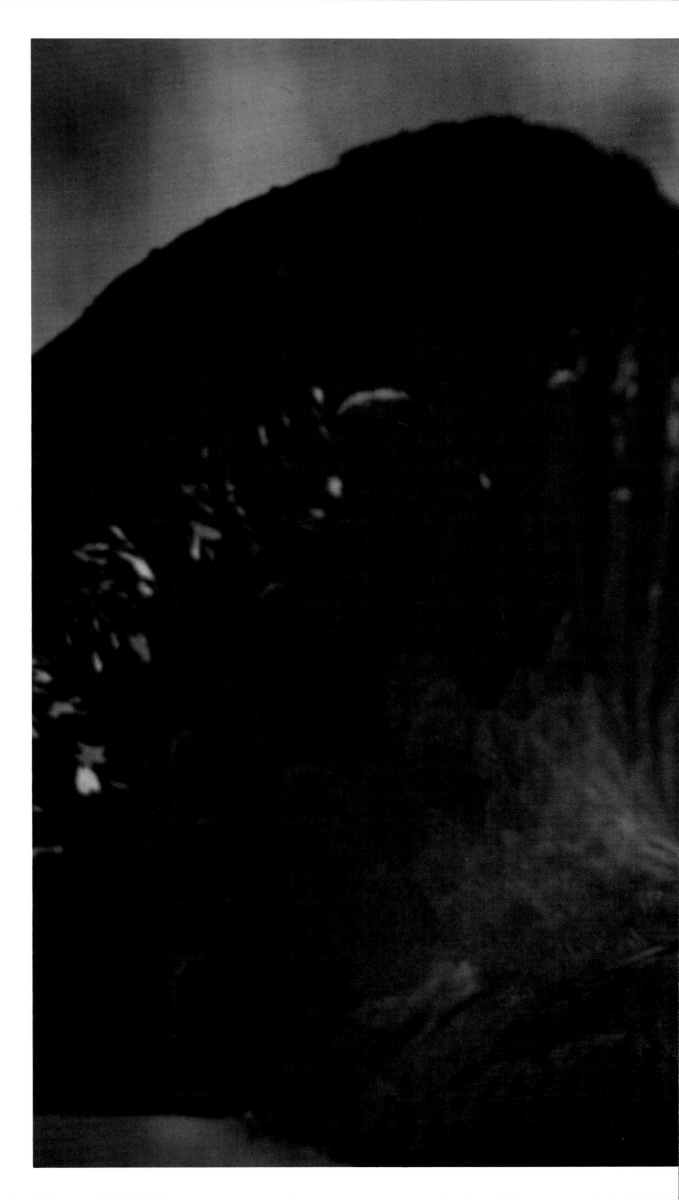

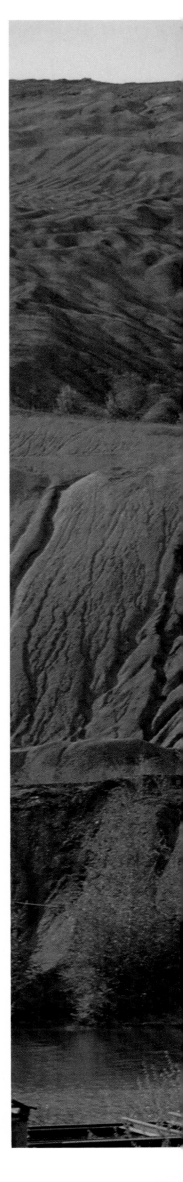

SÖDERMAN-LAND

The soul of a Sörmlander

Hubert is a cheerful citizen of Sörmland. He has curly, russet hair, good muscles, and mischief in his misleading blue eyes.

Hubert was conceived one rainy spring evening in a two-room flat with a spacious kitchen on Gotlandsgatan, in South Stockholm, when his parents were temporarily not quarreling, and the flat's other four paying guests were at the pictures. Valle and Martina declined to go and see Humphrey Bogart in the Maltese Falcon with the others that night, not so much because they had already seen it three times together, but because – since they weren't quarreling anymore and had a chance to get the flat to themselves – they were concerned to take the opportunity of making love all evening, without witnesses. It is true that Hubert's then four-year-old sister Lena was in the flat, but she was fast asleep in the kitchen after a full day's highly successful naughtiness. The result of that evening's amiability was Lena's brother, Hubert.

Hubert is now thirteen, and a highly civilized and harmonic young man for his age. He lives these days with Valle, Martina, Lena and his little brother Palle in an old, ornately carpentered, wooden house near Trångsund, south of Stockholm.

Let us accompany Hubert on a little walk. He wanders down to Freviken. There lies a raft, which the family built at Hubert's determined, not to say shrill, insistence when our hero was four.

Hubert paddles over the bay to Trångsund, and takes a walk through the woods. Here grow both pines and foliiferous trees. It's only six in the morning. Hubert encounters two roe deer, and exchanges a few words. Catching sight of a fox, Hubert stands still as a statue and observes. The fox also sees Hubert; but he does not turn tail, feeling a deep comradeship with the mini-fox that sits snickering behind Hubert's left ear.

Hubert picks en route a bunch of flowers for his buddy Orvar, who lives in Trångsund. He hopes that Orvar will have a girl with him, because then she will get the flowers. His bouquet consists of white and blue anenomes, hedge parsley, colt's foot, dandelions and a whole mass of attractive weeds. Hubert reflects during his walk that he could actually have paddled over to Finland on his raft, had he been in the mood. He decides also that if Orvar doesn't have a girl with him, then Orvar can have the flowers himself, provided he tells him the best way to paddle down through Europe.

by Einar Heckscher

STOCKHOLM

My mates in "South"
She lives in a flat in "South", the Swedish equivalent of London's Elephant and Castle, where Tompa, Tickan, Fredrik, Ubbe and the other genuine "Southerners" lived before they built their villas in Orminge, Sorunda and Saltsjöbaden, or bought flats in Östermalm and Kungsholmen.

Tompa, a genuine "Southerner", brought-up in the 50s in a little two-roomed flat in Skånegatan, still works his behind off, competes in the "Round Gotland Race", watches the Hammarby football team whenever it is playing at home, shoots moose, fishes, and re-members his old mates by giving them a life-buoy when they achieve their "40 antlers", with the inscription "Swim with the current, life starts at 40". Tompa has built up a computer service company, lives a life of stress with ten or so employees, is happily married for the fourth time, and has a nine-room flat in Kungsholmen.

Tickan, Tompa's great buddy when they were kids, is still giving him the same advice: "When a bird starts get-ting difficult, throw in the towel and get yourself a new one". Tickan got to be a folk-singer, poet and philosopher, and is now living with his seventh co-habiting lady in Orminge, a satellite community to the south.

Fredrik, another genuine "South-erner", although actually born a stone's throw south of Skanstull, made his money in the 70s on the idea of his PR and advertising company, "We'll fix it". After a fabulous flop with the publica-tion of square gramophone records, he sold all his status symbols and bought a little farm outside Sorunda, where he breeds trotting-horses.

Fredrik's new slogan, his mates just have to put up with: "You have to play it cool!". Then he adds, as usual: "I mean, I did get them to rent the entire City Hall to introduce the new square dance, and I actually got them to pro-duce square records". But only occa-sionally does he nowadays park his Porsche alongside the queue outside Stockholm's Café Opera.

Ubbe, who grew up on Hornsgatan in a home without either radio or tele-phone, got to be a work addict and building contractor; he still goes to work at five every morning, eats a banger around nine, and rarely gets home before eight at night. All on the excuse that "Work is where it's at lads, if I wasn't out there hammering in the nails myself I could never afford the house in Saltsjöbaden".

Some things, all my old mates from "South" have in common. They are all hungry, proud, straight-dealing and honest mates, whom some people regard as slightly eccentric.

And then, one day, I fell in love with one of South's new inhabitants.

She lives near the Slussen spaghetti junction, in a little two-roomed flat in Skånegatan; her eyes are deep as starflowers, and she is delicious—any book for the guidance of mushroom-pickers would award her three stars.

She has a great deal in common with the "Southerners" I have got to know. A hungry, proud, straight-dealing and honest lass, whom some people might regard as eccentric.

She comes from Värmland; she loves flowers and bees, and is bringing "South" to life again.

Stig Tjernquist

You sat there
Sat in that sweater
Made out of remnants
With nowhere to run to
    No matter how things go
You feel new
New when you wake up
New when a path is opened

I sat there
Sat in the sail boat
Holding your hand
Touching your lips
    No matter how things go
You feel new
New when you wake up
New when a door is opened

We sat there
Sat on the bare rock
And I kissed your lips
Caressed your body
    No matter how things go
You feel new
New when you wake up
New when a love is opened

We'll meet again
Meet by a fireside
I'll catch your eye
And warm your body
    No matter how things go
You feel new
New when you wake up
New when you're opened to love

by Stig Tjernquist

"There's nothing as cold as brick"
"Snow's for kids, and people who ski".
Or so the old man used to say, who sold newspapers at the corner of Hornsgatan and Varvsgatan, dressed in a cloth cap with ear-flaps and a grey shawl on top, a long black coat, and straw slippers. Beneath his coat he had three pullovers of different colours, you could see them all through the holes.

But his best source of warmth was his glowing hatred. He detested the winter. He stood there with the snow eddying around his legs, longing for the warmth of the Shipyard Café. His fingertips were a blueish-red in his half-mittens, which were to become the fashion 50 years later.

It's that long ago. So long ago that it was even before the Pale Negro, exhausted by life and drink, passed peacefully away in one of the snow-drifts in Högalid Park, to be discovered hard and pale as marble; he was the subject of discussion around the tables of Hornstull's beer-halls for at least a week.

All this was at a time when the snow in Stockholm lay white for many a day, and the hearts of the unemployed filled with hope when they looked up to the grey sky in the morning and saw the white gold spinning down. Because snow meant money.

From early morning until late at night they would then stand in long rows along the pavements, hacking away ice; all of them dressed in shiny cheviot suits, and cracked patent-Leather shoes, because their Sunday clothes were always the last to go.

It is so long ago that the city was still in the charge of people, the cars had not yet taken over.

"There's nothing as cold as brick", the old man with the newspapers used to say. To him the city was brick. He was longing, one assumes, for a red-painted wooden cabin at the edge of the forest, with snow-laden fir trees, a little home with a kitchen, and a spindle-back chair in front of a glowing iron stove.

Nowadays, too, we Stockholmers wade through our streets, but no longer in white snow. We wade through a dirt-coloured muck that we probably wouldn't dare look at even, if we got a chemical analysis in our hands. And the snow falling from the roofs is brown…

And yet, the city has its days.

When the sun shines over the people jigging for fish in Riddarfjärden. When the ski tracks shine blue over the ice of Årstaviken. When the temperature and humidity collaborate, and turn our statues to silver. When we set virgin footsteps in the untouched white of Allmänna Gränd, where the laughter, the shouts and the cursing have frozen into silence outside the Gröna Lund fun-fair.

I suppose he was right, the newspaper vendor, when he said that there's nothing as cold as brick. But we who walk the city with damp feet and dripping noses know that there's nothing as warm as brick either. In the summers. But that, as they say, is another story…
by Ove Magnusson

Old Town

My love of the Old Town, and my allegiance to it, were something I long kept secret. Something I was ashamed of.

I was born there—in the late 20s—and at that time this was no cause to put on airs. For four years the world outside my home was the area around Köpmantorget. The view from my window took in Nötkes "St. George and the Dragon", the Pilsener drinkers who seemed to have established permanent domicile on the stone bench in front of the statue, and, in the background, Köpmangatan—"Merchant Street"—Stockholm's oldest street-name, dating from 1323.

My memories are vague, fragmentary. I need the assistance of smells, sounds, the recollections of older brothers and sisters, for images to come to life. Neither Bellman nor Taube jog my memory. But a few lines from Ivar Lo-Johansson's "The Stockholmer" will take me back fifty years in the space of seconds.

"The island of the Old Town contained a brew of contradictions. Primaeval odours rose from the sewer gratings. Down by the water there was a fragrance of tar, of the harbour. The steamers emitted a smell of cold steam. In among the alleyways lived a human conglomerate, with swarms of kids. Victrolas like overgrown pot-plants screamed from the open, slanting windows. A penny cinema was running a Wild Western. Dockers stood bargaining with chest-high matrons for illegal spirits, or more seldom love".

Today the "human conglomerate" is made up of tourists, the swarms of kids are classes of visiting schoolchildren. And if anyone is still ashamed of living in the Old Town, it is certainly not on the grounds of indigence.

Such are my thoughts today as I saunter along Köpmangatan and Österlånggatan, as they wind their way along like the footpaths they once were.

Many years later I was to re-encounter the throng of humanity, the swarms of kids, the music blaring from open windows, and the primaeval odours. When I visited Rome, and the narrow streets of Trastevere. And I felt that I had come home. The Renaissance buildings of Rome were also something *déja vu:* I was seeing in them, once more, Tessin's and Oxenstierna's Royal Palace in Stockholm.

I put the Old Town at the top of my list once when I was to play guide to an old Italien friend, on his first visit to Stockholm. He came, he saw, and was pretty reserved about the whole thing. But this was just like home, in the mediaeval town where he was born in North Italy!

No, the new town was what he wanted. Those five gleaming excavation marks—the then newly built skyscrapers by Sergels Torg—sent him into raptures.

by Britt Ågren

Swedish Steam Day

"Swedish Steam Day" is the popular label given to the grand "review" put on since the mid 1960s by the steamers plying in the Stockholm archipelago, on the first Wednesday in June each summer. The occasion's official designation is "Archipelago Boat Day", and it is arranged by the Archipelago Traffic Association in cooperation with the shipowners.

As island steamers are counted, naturally, also those plying between the islands in Lake Mälar. One of the most handsome vessels in this annual parade is thus the SS Mariefred, which has been plying the route between Stockholm and Mariefred since 1903. She is distinguished from the other vessels by her tall, plain black funnel, and by her bearing her name—painted in gold letters on her "chest".

The interesting thing is that these island-plying boats – those powered by steam – underwent a rebirth at the very instant in which they were about to die out. The great fleet of steamers that had sailed in the archipelago and on Lake Mälar since the turn of the century was in the process, in the late 40s and early 50s, of being briskly scrapped.

The official policy on public transport was to extend land communications as far as possible by means of bridges and embankments. The rest was to be handled by ferries and tenders. On the longer routes, there was no longer any place for these large, comfortable vessels.

At a time when practically all the steamers had disappeared, public opinion was suddenly aroused and the preservation was then fought against the rational thinkers, with their cold, strictly economic calculations. Every conceivable argument was mobilised: one of the most effective moves was the launching of the term "Steamboat Steak", for which, I suspect, I myself must bear the blame.

During the real era of the steamers, there was no such name. "Fried steak and onions" was all it said on the menu, insofar as this dish was on offer at all; nor was it surrounded by any particularly romantic aura. But for many of those concerned to save the steamers the phrase "Steamboat Steak", launched as it were almost posthumously, became something of a symbol for the now-lapsed and supremely desirable passenger traffic we wished to revive.

The campaign was successful, and it was a major achievement when Waxholmsbolaget – which was taken over in the early 50s by the County Council, and the public sector – decided to retain the steamers "Express II", "Orrskär", and "Storskär". The first of these was renamed the "Waxholm". This having been totally destroyed by fire one winter night some years ago, there remain only the "Norrskär" and the "Storskär", guarded now by public opinion as jealously as a dragon watches over a hoard of gold.

The only steamer left plying in Lake Mälar was the "Mariefred". Its future was secured in 1966 when the Archipelago Boats Foundation acquired a majority shareholding in the company that owns it. Two years later the Strömma Canal company was formed, under whose red emblem two further steamers, "Drottningholm" and "Björkfjärden", now operate in Lake Mälar.

In Saltsjön the same company operates also the "Gustavsberg VII". In addition to which we have the stately "SS Blidösund", owned and operated by a large group of steamer enthusiasts.

This gives us a total of seven steam-powered passenger ships. Two of these, the "Mariefred" and the "Blidösund", are fired by coal. In the others, the water in the boilers is heated by means of oil.

This knowledge cannot, however, allay my longstanding suspicion that these steamers are in fact fired by nothing less than steak ... How otherwise is one to explain the intensive odour of fried steak – blended with fresh cucumber and the fragrance of dill in the potato pot – that permeates these vessels day in, day out, whether under way or at anchor?

This odour reaches its peak of intensity precisely on Swedish Steam Day, just before the steamers put out from Strömkajen, blending with the coal smoke that drifts in heavy clouds over Kungsträdgården. Then, as the steam whistles blast off together to signal departure, the people of Stockholm know that yet another summer season of steam has commenced.

What the new season will bring with it by way of encounters, adventures, and windy hours on deck, no one knows. But one thing is certain: the risk of going aground has been drastically reduced since the first shoal on the route – that which used to lie between Strömkajen and the Logård Steps – has been blasted away. This was done on Swedish Steam Day itself, and dead smelt and Baltic herring floated to the surface in their masses. The trip this June evening is to Waxholm and back; which is entirely in accordance with the old Swedish saying that if we meet no more in this life, we will always meet – in Waxholm.

by Bo Grandien

THE STOCKHOLM ARCHIPELAGO

The land is still rising, 10 000 years after the inland ice disappeared. New shallows, new skerries, new harbours are being formed the whole time. While old channels are silting up. On the old "Crown Fisheries" skerries in the outermost archipelago, you can find rings and the remains of jetties far up on shore. And the Viking graves on Ingarö, now high up in the woods, once lay down by the sea.

There are villages and farms inland on Runmarö, where sheep graze in a meadow that was once a bay of the sea.

People have been living out here since the Middle Ages, farmers, skippers, fishermen, often all in one and the same person. Those living on the big islands in the Central Archipelago—Runmarö, Möja, Ornö—had small patches of arable land, and kept cows around their houses. In the summers, they set out for the fishing skerries in the outer archipelago. There they lived in whole villages of huts, which were so ramshackle that they blew away in the winter storms and had to be built up anew each summer.

In late August and early September, they rowed and sailed the long route into Stockholm, and sold salt herring and cod. They could row right up to Sigtuna and Uppsala, to barter fish for grain.

Different islands came to specialize in different livelihoods. On Svartlöga, they built the best sailing craft in all Roslagen. On Runmarö there lived only pilots, generation after generation.

You can meet an old man on Runmarö, and ask him how long he has lived there. "Since 1705," he will say, since he is a pilot and pilots, above all men, keep their family trees in order.

And then he starts castigating the Russians, who burned down the entire archipelago in the summer of 1719.

Some important changes occurred in people's way of life in the 1920s. The people on the Swedish mainland stopped eating Baltic herring, which is a delicacy, but had acquired over the years the label of "poor man's food".

An important source of livelihood for the islanders thus vanished; at the same time restrictions on alcohol, with an accompanying ration book, opened up new opportunities. The islanders painted their fishing boats grey, so that the Excise would not see them. And sailed out to sea, where the smacks with vodka from Esthonia and Poland awaited them at the 18-mile limit.

The running of liquor was both a blessing and a curse to the islanders: many of them grew rich, others drank away their money and their homes.

In some families, one son become a smuggler, another an Exciseman.

All this is history now: the Second World War put an end to the smuggling, and, as always in hard times, people began once more to eat Baltic herring.

Those living out here are still jacks-of-all-trades. They make their living by fishing, by freighting summer visitors between the islands and the mainland, and repairing houses and bridges for them.

More and more people have sailing boats, and many complaints are heard of the crowding out among the sker-ries. But there are 60 000 islands in the Stockholm archipelago—and there is no real need to sail to Sandhamn, where the boats nowadays are double and triple parked along the quay.

When learning to sail, it is perhaps advisable to stick to the safe islands of the inner archipelago, where there is protection from all winds, and the woods grow down to the shore.

In fact, the archipelago really begins in the heart of Stockholm, and it is quite an adventure to anchor up over night at Skeppsholmen and watch the sun go up over the Nordic Museum.

And Skeppsholmen was a little skerry even in Viking days.

But, obviously, people want to get furthest out. The Great Adventure starts when you have put the wooded islands behind you and are sailing out over open waters, and can see the outermost skerries rising like mirages on the horizon.

It's enough to lie up for a few days alone in some inlet out there, your boat surrounded by gentle warm faces of rock, hearing no other sounds than the cry of gulls, and the swell breaking on the reefs.

You will have lost your heart!

by Lars Westman

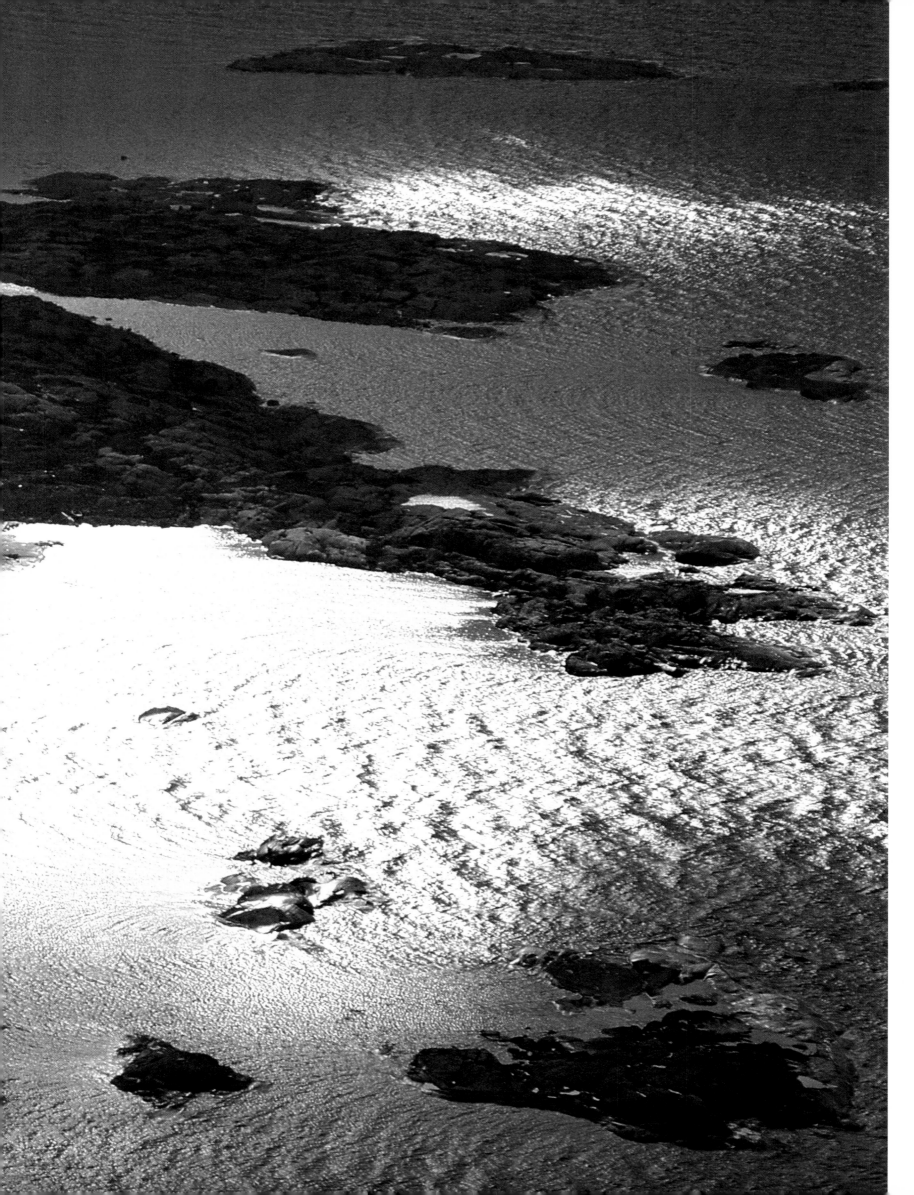

The road to salvation

In the old days of the sailing smacks, Korskobben ("Cross Rock") was their salvation when they came sailing in from the sea, and sighted it in a storm. It lies just off Storön in Svenska Högarna, where the approach to the emergency harbour used to run.

It was one of the most important sailing-marks along this part of the coast. The cairn, with its little cross, is indicated on a nautical chart dating from the 18th century. And those living on Högarna make sure that the cairn does not fall, and erect new crosses when the old ones have rotted.

But there is no longer any channel from Svenska Högarna in towards land. There was a pilot station out here once, but it terminated more or less of its own accord, as fewer and fewer ships took this route.

When there was a fog, a cannon was fired off up by the lighthouse, once every quarter of an hour. During the war, this was the destination of masses of small craft containing refugees from Esthonia and Latvia. Korskobben and Svenska Högarna were the first they saw of Sweden.

Now the ships pass far out to sea, well outside the old Rock and Svenska Högarna. And many of the old sailing-marks have become historic monuments, maintained mainly out of piety. Even the lighthouse on Svenska Högarna is now reduced to a coastal beacon, of no practical importance. The same is true of Huvudskär further south, where there also used to be an approach to Stockholm.

But the cairn and the cross out there on the Rock remain to remind us how things were not all that long ago. Only 50 years ago, three-masted barks could be seen lying in the emergency harbour at Högarna.

In the summers, amateur divers arrive looking for wrecks out here on the shoals.

And on the rocks in the emergency harbour itself remain a few rusty rings, cast in lead.

So in this picture, we should imagine a heeling smack on its way in from the open sea, in to salvation.

by Lars Westman

UPPLAND

The blow struck the middle of his neck, and he fell prone without a sound. A chronicler with less stylistic feeling might have written that he "bit the grass". Because when they found the chieftain's son, he was lying face down in the Uppland summer meadow, among the almond blossom and forget-me-nots as if he were smelling the flowers. A blackbird sung in the hazel thicket, and flies hummed around the sword-cut in his neck, where the blood had congealed.

When they carried in the dead man, the chieftain said not a word. He continued to sit immobile on his seat of honour, just as they had seen him throughout his time of office: bald, broad, with a sulkily protruding lower lip, and large pale-blue eyes that mirrored the sky over the plains, or perhaps the Baltic Sea on which he had sailed as a young man.

A day later, the chieftain called for his most trusted men. "My son is to be buried beside his grandfather", he said, "in the mound across the plain. But let us now go to the place where my son was slain.".

The meadow sloped down to the lake. The sunlight sifted down through the shimmering leafy vaults of the birch trees. This, the son had been accustomed to say, was the most attractive spot on the estate, the fairest place in Uppland. Here, he had often walked in solitude. Which had been his undoing. The chieftain stood looking out over the bay, to the woods on the other side. "This is to be a holy place," he said to the pagan priest beside him. "Let it be consecrated to Njord for all future time. Protect it from intrusion. No sacrifices shall be made here, other than to Fertility each summer. Otherwise let peace and stillness prevail".

The blow was aimed at the chin, but glanced off because its deliverer was by no means sober. The young lad fell backwards over a table, at which two fat teenagers were stuffing down their fourth hot-dog. The one, who now had mustard all over his white jeans — which his mother had scrubbed clean only the previous evening — swore angrily; but the young man who had been felled heard nothing, since the waves of sound from the rock band on stage were so powerful as to render all speech dumb, mouth movements in the warm summer evening. Some time previously a gang of motorcyclists had tried to take the People's Park by storm; now, wise from previously demolished fencing and overturned stalls, the park management had called in police reinforcements, and repulsed the attack. The manager of the People's Park himself was seated, as usual, at a table behind the lottery stall. He was bald, broad, with a surlily protruding lower lip. He said very little. His large pale-blue eyes mirrored the sky, or perhaps the soft drink in the bottle in front of him, a concoction labelled "Berries of the Forest".

Behind the dance-floor, the meadow sloped down to the lake. An entwined couple tacked their way between the birch-trees. After the rock band's punk version of the latest Eurovision Song Contest winner, which put the few moose remaining in the nearest 50 square miles to flight, he had dragged her with him between the clusters of screaming 14-years-olds; and now they sank down in the grass, among the almond blossom and forget-me-nots. She looked out over the lake. Dawn was already breaking, and a blackbird began to sing in a thicket of hazel. The rock band had stopped playing.

"It's so beautiful here", she said. "It must be the most beautiful place in the world. Or at least in Uppland". But he didn't answer, he was already asleep.

by Finn Zetterholm

VÄSTMAN-
LAND

He limped down into the Vale of
Flowers, which in reality was just a tiny
hollow in the landscape, and when he
finally reached the swaying bank of the
River Järle, looked out over its foaming
waters as they sped past, and
breathed in the tangy air, slightly cooled
now by the evening, he was perfectly
happy, apart from the fact that his broken leg ached, and his old-fashioned
crutches had flayed his armpits in the
course of the day.

It was late spring, or perhaps early
summer. And the spring flood that was
usually so capricious and brutal, had
long since poured through the old
smithy at Järle Hammar, not taking with
it a single plank.

He tottered a few steps along the
shore, and sank into the new, tender
grass between two whispering alders;
from the Vale of Flowers came a sym-
phony of scents from the entire flora of
the province, which lay thick on the
fertile ground. It occurred to him that
even the lime-worts and hedge parsley
were different in this place, reaching
up to heaven with almost absurd self-
confidence.

Some dippers dived into the eddying
waters, and it was some time before
they reappeared. In his mind, he could
see them scouring the stony riverbed,
holding their breath, in search of the
edible.

Earlier in the day, he had been out
with the Old Man and the big black
dog in the unspoiled forests a few miles
south of the river. This was the Old
Man's forest, and it would remain for
as long as he survived; and perhaps
even much longer, even if the forestry
companies were out clawing sunder
the entire terrain round about.

"We can't do without the forests,"
the Old Man muttered as they stood
there on a shoulder of rock, strewn with
strange mosses and lichens. "When
the forests have all gone, Man is des-
tined to disappear."

At early, dew-drenched dawn, they
had cautiously crept their way to the
upper reaches of the river, where dili-
gent beavers swam to and fro in the
pockets of calm water between their
dwellings. Everywhere along the banks
they had felled trees of all sizes.

"But this," said the Old Man delight-
edly, "is legal felling, so to speak. The
beavers have a licence from God to fell
trees. And that's nothing that we poor
sinners have any right to change."

The black dog regarded the beavers
with suspicion, and dipped a fore paw
in the water, but realized that it was too
cold. Otherwise, this was a young, busy
and inquisitive dog who had almost
forgotten having tried his paws on a
large hedgehog the previous year.

As they proceeded slowly down
stream again, his leg throbbed worse
than ever, but he ignored it as he knew
that he would otherwise be unable to
keep up even with the Old Man's pace.
The black dog seemed to sense it, and
tripped along at an angle behind him,
as if to be prepared should something
happen.

And now he stretched out between
the alders, and in the fragrant new
grass; and the sun was still high in the
sky, and a pigeon hawk circled thought-
fully above a little waterfall in midriver.
Over every living thing, there lay still a
bright, warm, softly shimmering Nordic
summer.

From the Valley of Flowers there suddenly emerged, with rolling gait,
a badger, who had scented the clear,
clear, fresh water.

by Anderz Harning

DALARNA

He sits on a rock amid the rushing waters—hardly visible, yet not concealing himself. His skin is as water and stone; a live creature, but surrounded by the chill of death that causes all life in the stream, and in the bushes along its shores, to fall silent, and flee.

He listens, through the rushing of the waters, to the music from the village. They have been dancing there all day, and half way through the night; the fiddlers have played without cease, the one tune after the other.

First, the music had been mild and friendly. People danced in a ring around the garlanded Maypole, and the sun was high in the sky. Towards evening, as the fiddlers and dancers moved into the barn, the mood changed. The fiddle no longer sung only of joy, and sunshine, but also of melancholy, and longing.

The swirl of country dances, elated laughter and shouting, strong arms around supple waists: they could have danced forever, but even the most festive occasion must sometime come to an end.

Two by two, they wandered out into the bright, cool night. Rosy-cheeked and light-headed after the dancing, warm, glowing, and still unwilling to part. The old, the wise, went home to bed, their minds turning to the morrow. Those bent more on continued flirtation, and kissing than on sleep, wandered towards the hill-top to see the dawn break.

Last of all came the fiddler, his fiddle silent beneath his arm.

And in the rushing waters sits the Neck, the Water Sprite, still immobile, listening intensively into the night, and the silence. Another Midsummer Eve has passed, but the unrest still tears at his heart. Never is his own darkness greater than in this bright night, no more than a brief, still pause between sunset and dawn.

The music from the barn was a faint echo of his own music. In it, he heard his own longing, his strength, the wild waters, the swaying birches.

It was his music, the music of the Neck. He had given it to mankind, in exchange for the lives of young maidens, or the soul of a fiddler. And now he raises his own fiddle and plays. He is strong, and his music casts a blinding spell; with it, he can entice any creature down into the cold waters of the river. His strength condemns him to solitude; he despises the weakness of mortals, even as he longs to share it.

The wind carries his haunting, dangerous melody up to the hill…

A young girl stops, lingering behind the others.

"Come now," says her true love, offering his hand and his desire.
"You go on," she answers. "I'll catch you up in a moment."

He smiles, and moves on. He can afford to be patient, knowing that she will soon rejoin him.

She finds herself walking slowly towards the river, and wonders why. Then she gives a sudden smile, and wants to embrace herself and all living creatures in this strange night. With brisk steps, she finds the path down to the waterfall. "I'll just dip my feet in the water," she says to herself.

"And then I'll catch up with the others."

by Åsa Lind

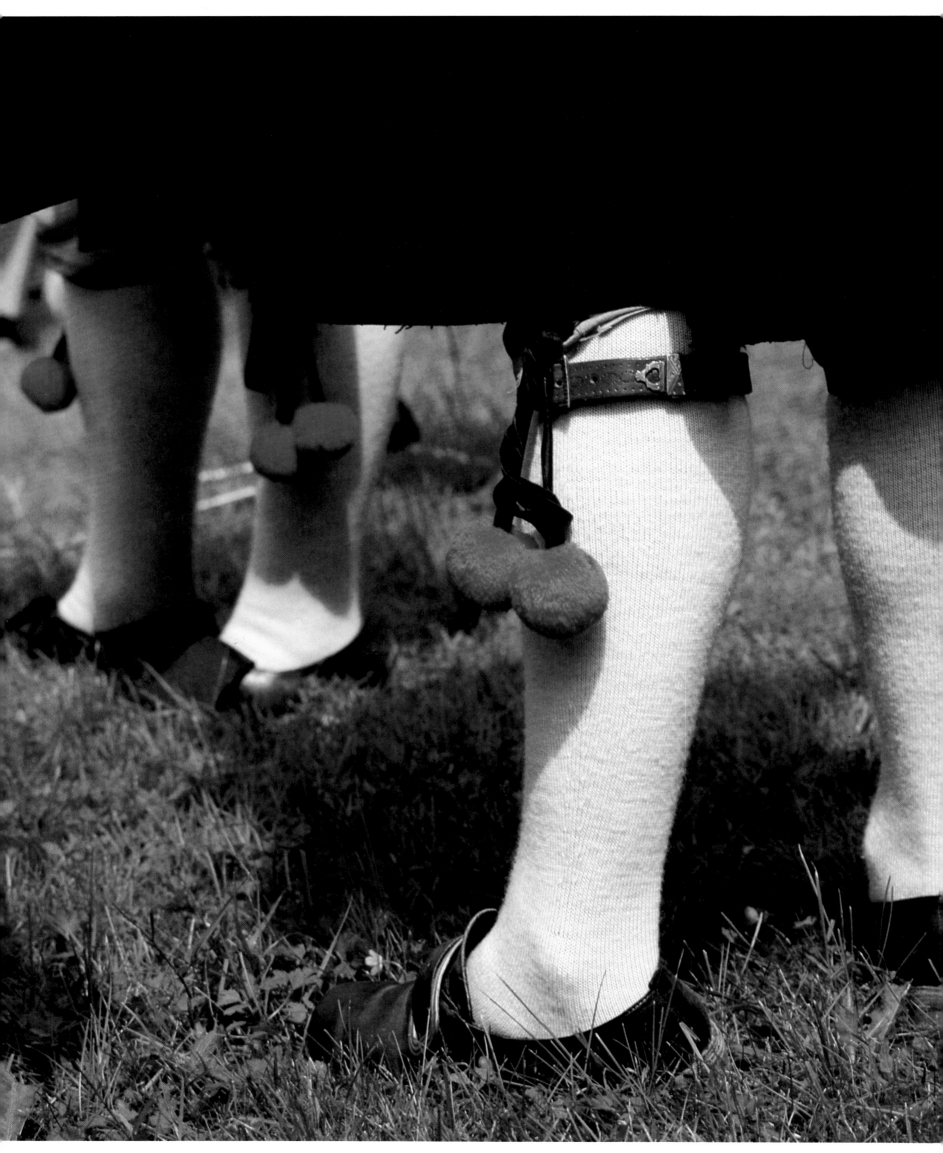

The "Big Bake" and dairyfarm bread

The bakehouse was hot and crowded. The air was filled with the talk and laughter of the women, the clouds of flour, and the fragrance of freshly baked bread. The stones in the oven glowed red.

The "Bake" continued for several days, but then the bread was to suffice for half a year. First they baked the thin, coarse everyday bread, which could be hung from the ceiling to dry out and "hay itself" for an indefinite period. When the oven had cooled slightly, it was time for the "feast-baking": sweet loaves, left to rise high, and flavoured with aniseed and fennel; these were brought out at weddings, and at Christmas.

In the summer, the people at the outlying dairy farms often baked, on top of the stove, a bread that can be eaten to advantage with newly churned butter and goat's-milk cheese.

Dairyfarm bread

Pass one kilo of boiled, peeled potatoes through a meat grinder together with one teaspoonful salt. Knead together with three coffee cups of rye flour into a hard dough. Roll out into paper-thin "cakes" and prick with a fork. Cook in a pancake pan on top of the stove. (A mixer also gives excellent results!)

by Åsa Lind

A story from Siljan

No, he was no beauty, Björn-Jon. He was, to tell the truth, appallingly ugly, even on a day like this when he had bathed, and donned his best clothes. He'd been ugly when he first saw the light of day, and hard years as a hunter and charcoal burner had lent something black and matted to his crouched figure.

That his heart was warm and generous, that his innermost being was pure love, this was not easy to read from his exterior. The stubborness, however, was clearly written in his unyielding gaze.

Many an eye followed his path through the village. His business was known to everyone; indeed, Björn-Jon himself had told all enquirers that he had returned to the village of his childhood to ask for the hand of Persbonden's daughter.

And that, as Persbonden remarked, was tantamount to swearing in church.

"How dare that misshapen bearhunter even think of my Kristina?"

Persbonden was quivering with wrath. His Kristina, his only daughter, was the sweetest and loveliest maiden in all Siljan.

"But," he added generously, "let her decide for herself!"

And so the stiff-necked hunter stood before the rich farmer. Unfalteringly, Jon made it clear to the farmer that he desired Kristina's hand in marriage. Persbonden replied, as he had promised, that the girl should decide for herself, but he did nothing to conceal his scorn.

Pale, and moved by the drama of the moment, Kristina came to meet Jon. They spoke together on the sward, before the eyes of all, but beyond the reach of inquisitive ears.

No one knows what was said. Kristina returned to her father, still paler, if that were possible, than before.

"I have given him a year," was all she said. "He is to build me a manorhouse."

And Jon started building.

Down by the lake, on his father's land, he built a manor-house, a castle for his princess. All was scrupulously prepared, and calculated. He had had plenty of time to think during his lonely evenings in foresters' cabins, and all that he had earned from his dealings in hides, and at the charcoal-stacks, he had saved for this building.

Before the year was at an end, the house was ready. With the front stoop facing south, and the back wall against the north wind, as was right and proper. With stables and threshing-house, cattle-sheds and larder - all in their right places, and built with obstinacy and love.

Kristina, who had silently watched his work, log by log, saw confirmed what she had sensed in her only talk with Jon - there was, in him, a rare force, and an immeasurable love.

She noticed his ugliness less and less.

Despite Persbonden's oaths and fury, Jon and Kristina were wedded. They lived together all their days in their palace, and their children, fortunately, were blessed with their mother's beauty and their father's strength. What else was to be expected from such a happy tale?

And it seemed, in fact, to the villagers, that Jon grew less and less ugly over the years.

But perhaps they just got used to him.

by Åsa Lind

GÄSTRIKLAND

It had been raining the whole afternoon, and the lingonberry brushwood had drenched his trousers up to the knees; the moss was wet and slippery, as he made his way down to the little eddying stream and suddenly found himself looking into the eyes of Old Ben.

This was his life's second bear. The first he had encountered 25 years previously, far up in the north, at an age when he had felt (and to some extent been) like Faulkner's young lad Isaac McCaslin. On this occasion, he was a bit of both Major de Spain and old Boon Hogganbeck, or even Sam Fathers. It was just that, deep down, he was older and tireder than all of them.

As always, he was wearing a pair of brown slippers. There were holes in both their cork soles, and the water seeped in under the weight of his 125 kilos; his five numbers too small jeans jacket from his days as Isaac McCaslin hung loosely over his shoulders, and in his one hand he held as usual his light, telescope rod, with its short line, and hook at the ready. A few minutes previously, he had not even known of this stream, so deeply incised was it in the dense, old forest.

Old Ben was large, but not as large as one might have imagined. He was a solid, grey-brown bear, whom this encounter had obviously taken by surprise. The faint wind blew from his direction, and he stood as it were suspended over his front paws, an astonished expression on his face. In between them, the stream eddied. It occurred to him that Old Ben had probably emerged from the virgin forest like this at early dusk in order to drink.

Then he saw the fresh tracks in the sandy bed right beside him, at the narrowest point of the stream. The bear had crossed the stream only a minute or so before, and now it was raising its heavy head and stretching its neck.

As on that first occasion, so many years ago, he was overcome by an incredibly triumphant, hot feeling that burned through his blood, his head, his heart. This was a joy utterly naked, undivided, and perfect, in which his dream of Old Ben had finally merged into Old Ben himself, and all that the bear represented in the past, the present, and the dubious future.

"I've been waiting for you, bear," he said quietly.

His slippers splashed, as he carefully lifted them from the wet moss. Old Ben was still leaning forward over his paws, obviously worried over what attitude to adopt. This human being, after all, was on the other side of the stream. He was difficult to attack, and nothing to run from. That thin thing he was carrying under one paw didn't look especially dangerous.

Slowly, Old Ben loped a few yards away from the brink of the stream; then he stopped, turning his head back towards the man, who was standing immobile in the same place. The rain had almost stopped, and the darkness was streaming in over the deep, old forest. For a dizzying moment, it suddenly felt as if there were some unexpressed understanding between them. Old Ben threw a last look at the human being, and then melted slowly in among the trees. Just then, and perhaps for the last time, he was young Isaac McCaslin. He cupped his hand and drank the water from the stream, which tasted of mould, and marsh, and magnesium.

by Anderz Harning

HÄLSING-LAND

They drove up over the hog-backs on an old forest road, with the unbelievable landscape all around them. A moose, and her two calves, stood still as statues in a cleared area of forest. A roe-deer gyrated out of their path, leaping high. Some hares vanished over an old burn-beaten clearing, watched by a patient goshawk resting on the thermals. A fox cub who had not yet been destroyed by the scab tumbled playfully around on a slope down towards a deep lake, the black surface of which was constantly broken by salmon-trout. The last swallows, having raised two broods during the hot summer, swung themselves in waves up into the sky. "This is the place", she said suddenly, "I can feel it". She started busying herself with her Lapp bag and picker and sandwiches and cigarettes.

"Stop just here, would you?"

The road skirted a velvet-black tarn that smelled of sedge and horsetail and mouldering cloudberries. Some ancient aspens, with grey-black trunks and shimmering foliage breathed quietly in the hot Indian summer. A few slim birches had found their way in among the fir-trees. Beyond the tarn began the great, deep marshland, where knotted dwarf pines twisted toward the sky. It would soon be autumn in Hälsingland, and he was longing for the pink and violet and bright red colours, and the first intimation of approaching snow.

"It must be here", she muttered, and got out of the car beside a great rowan-tree which was sputtering clusters of ripe fruit.

And as the woman he loved slipped into the forest, he could still sense the fragrance of her rich soft hair, which shone like old Turkish copper in the sun.

"There's the lot here", she called. "We'll have lingonberry, and bog-berry, and rowanberry!"

Before she vanished in among the trees, the words of the Song of Soloman ran through his head:

"O Prince's daughter! The joints of thy thighs are like jewels, the work of the hands of a cunning workman.

"Thy navel is like a round goblet, which wanteth not liquor: thy belly is like a heap of wheat set about with lillies. Thy two breasts are like two young roes that are twins."

It was as if voices from the time before time were singing the praises of just his woman, just his countryside.

During the afternoon, he darted across the hills and down through the valleys, trying all the streams. He knew from experience that the most innocent-looking water courses held the most salmon-trout. The best stream was about half a metre broad, and about a decimetre deep. It meandered, unbroached, through the wild countryside.

Dusk fell quickly, and she had still not emerged from the forests. When the grey turned to pitch black, he gathered his friends to help search. He saw her, in his mind, lost and groping in the darkness. But just as his mind had turned to all the wild creatures that prowled in the black night, there she suddenly stood once more on the forest road, her Lapp bags brimming, and a wild flower behind her left ear. "And what are you doing out in the wilds this late?" she enquired in mild reproach.

"You could get lost." When he kissed her, dancing, she tasted of wood-sorrel and late summer.   *by Anderz Harning*

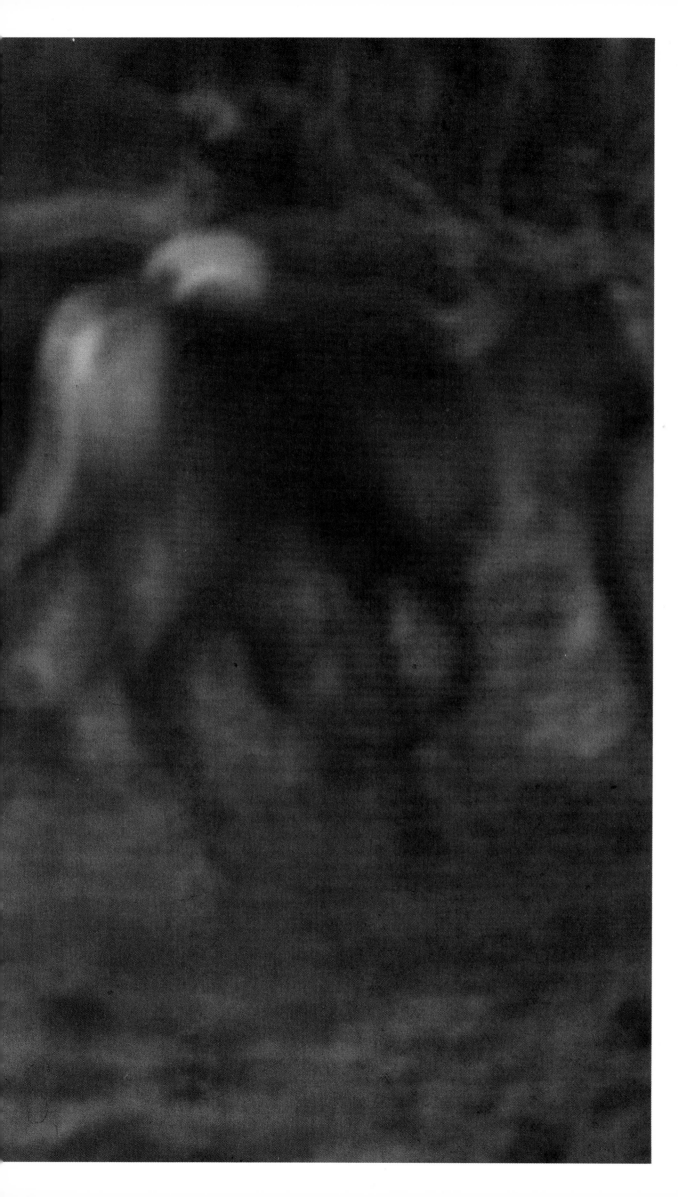

HÄRJEDALEN

The river is the haze and the mist and life flowing by.

But the river is also the life that constantly returns. The curlew crying over the meadows along its banks. The great cranes screaming to all and sundry that "now we're off." Off to our summer territories; now the broad sun is back, and the yellow-green foliage. Now the fens in the remotest fells are graced with the delicate greenery of high summer.

The river links together the long lakes.

Ribbons of fields, a thousand years old. And natural cairns—stones that have eaten their way up from the entrails of our Nordic earth. Beneath the plough, beneath the herds of calves, these stones eat their way from the elfin kingdom up to the bright lights of early summer. Out from the meagre soil.

The frost in the Vale of Water was watched over by timbered dwellings. From the slopes down to the lakes, windows spied out over the landscape. From the hog-back, eyes followed the cloud formations of the blight on the crops.

Under the yellow eye of the owl, pines were felled. To become pit props in the mines of Britain.

A thousand years after the Byzantine coinage was introduced, the forests and the water became our falls, running down to the world at large. The farmer and his hand abandoned their journeys to Stockholm, where they had traded in hides and game. They readjusted their lives to become forest workers, and building labourers for the hydro-electric plants. They were readjusted by the coinage. Their lives proceeded according to business cycles, and crashes on the Stock Exchange of the world.

And people took the forests. And they took the power. The purchasers of raw materials are laying dry watercourses, submerging valleys, ploughing the forests, slashing at the mountainsides.

How many years have passed since Englishmen, out for grouse, first shot the silence to pieces? . . . A time to be recalled with a sense, almost, of comfort.

As the twentieth century slopes towards its close, we may, temporarily, spell ourselves out as 'ski lift operators' or 'suppliers of raw materials'. But one day even the IMF will find itself in a museum, in a stand beside the Byzantine coinage. Near a pair of modest ski-boots.

The river is live . . . as it comes and goes . . . The opportunities that have vanished . . .

The metallic jarring of the raven over the island. The tails of the white mountain cows, lashing out at insects. The hooves of reindeer picking in the moorland that is their winter pasture.

A human fist, the warmth of a human cheek.

The laughter, as spring approaches.

And the deep security of a pine, as it stands, rusty brown, among the pebbles of the lake shore, lifting its branches like the antlers of a moose over the Vale of Water.

by Peter Moskin

JÄMTLAND

The people of Jämtland

"What's up with him then?" I wondered, observing him long and carefully from different angles. He seemed to me a bundle of silent protest. "The withdrawn type," I concluded. The sort who always had his mouth tucked out of sight.

"Just a dour Jämtlander," someone said. Could that be the answer? Any cross-grained, taciturn person can be called "dour". I assumed that a talent of this sort might run in a family, but could the entire province of Jämtland be inhabited by the same sort of folk?

Well, there might after all be something in that story of what hell is like, with the English doing the cooking and the Germans telling the jokes, I thought. And continued to observe my subject, who could best be described as obviously capable of sulking his way to various advantages. Someone who used his silence to pressure those around him.

People on the whole detest such characters. I am one of the exceptions. I am delighted when people fail to respond to a cordial approach, and just give you a long, searching look. Their distrust gives me a colossal kick.

Dead smart, I think, to instill in your partner-opponent a vague sense of failure. Dead smart to entice other people into offering still more. Which is what you do, when you feel you have failed. Right?

As far as I'm concerned, they can be as mean as they please. That's their business. But *I* benefit from having to raise the level and quality of my own generosity. Surly people may not be restful, but they do make you feel secure. They won't make the tiniest little positive gesture, without having tried and tested every aspect of the situation. So when they finally decide you may be worth a little confidence, it's worth gold. Their confidence is based on rock, not on sand. An actual smile, for example, is something so rare that you feel one of the chosen few, a rich person.

And that's the point. When a dour Jämtlander smiles, you feel as if you had won the pools. I think that's dead smart.

Whether they're consciously up to no good is more than I can say.
by Loka Enmark

MEDELPAD

One brightly shining August morning in what (did he but know it) was the Year of Grace 606, Thorfinn Throatcut sat on the sward in Högom picking his teeth with Redslay, his beloved spear. From time to time, he would turn his great shaggy head to cast a satisfied glance down at his newly built little eight-oar craft, idly bobbing in the faint breeze that crimped the sun-glittering sea.

Little did he imagine that fields of golden wheat would centuries later billow over his favourite fishing grounds. He can hardly, after all, have known anything of land elevation, even if he had sensed, over practically a life-span, that the water seemed somehow to be withdrawing.

Thorfinn shuddered, and turned his eyes inside out, every time Redslay touched one of the incisors in his lower jaw. He felt old and weak; that very morning, he had been obliged to sneak stealthily off with a leg of mutton, which his toothache had prevented him from biting off.

He had tried absolutely everything, except, of course, a shameful visit to the swordsmith, who was known for his brutal but efficient way with ageing jaws. Thorfinn felt, quite simply, that he could not stand the local gossip. He could hear in his mind the old women whispering about the old boar, who ought to be put away, and not allowed to become a burden to the community.

Valhalla seemed to have stopped listening to his prayers. And yet, at dusk last evening, he had cloven two slaves from what is now called Dalarna with his sacrificial scythe. He had cloven them standing, from top to bottom, as in the old days: only with one of them, he had had to twist his scythe a bit to get the iron through the body. This had never happened before. He hoped that no one had observed his little deceit at the place of sacrifice. Things were not made better by the fact that slaves from that part of the country were traditionally regarded as of weak and splenic flesh.

But Valhalla, of course, had seen. There they were unlikely to forgive a man from this coast of heroes and berserks who couldn't even carve some flabby-fleshed knave from Västerskog.

Never more would Thorfinn Throatcut snap the windpipe of a 30-antlered bull moose with his front teeth. Never more would he flay a full-grown bear alive. Gone were the glorious days of his manhood, when he would without difficulty swallow a grey hen, feathers and death-cry and all.

Yet still the thicker of his veins began to throb, as he saw the forward-bending figure of Hewmaiden, his woman, proceeding through the barley. Absentmindedly, he laid aside his spear, stuffed a fistful of bilberries into his mouth, and inflated his thorax to the male position; red-faced and panting, he was about to rush down into the barley-field with a view, if possible, to replenishing the family ranks, when he was struck by the Light. He stopped in his tracks, smiling up at the clear blue sky.

Thorfinn Throatcut had a reputation for the Light. In this Light, he had often seen visions which had contributed to human progress: his gut-screw, for example, was known far and wide, and could get any man to confess to anything.

But on this August morning in the Year of Grace 606, standing on the sward of Högom, he invented *bilberry porridge.*

"Hewmaiden!" he shouted with stentorian voice. "Eight full fistfuls of bilberries, to be boiled to pieces. Then, slowly, beat in the finest barley. Two-rowed or six-rowed, no matter. And when it's thickened, and there are no lumps, we can eat!"

And so this divine Medelpad speciality was created. Thorfinn Throatcut rapidly forgot that he had created it because it was easy to chew.

Centuries later, the peoples of all the dark regions to the south started lapping up "bilberry fool", which presupposes potato-flour. But there are still folk along the coast of heroes who start thumbing their sacrificial scythes when the sub-humans of those barbarous provinces imagine that bilberry porridge and bilberry fool are the same thing!

by Anderz Harning

ÅNGERMANLAND

"I could a tale unfold," said the ancient Baltic herring, as he stood gaping in the Bothnian, just east of the Högbonden beacon.

"I could a tale unfold …

"Of the way things were, and the way things are …"

In fact he was a perfectly ordinary herring, being almost 35 cm in length; he had been south of Öland, and swum with the big boys and girls in the Atlantic, and elsewater.

But he preferred the title of "Baltic"; it reminded him of his happy childhood, from the time he had been a cheerful little grain of roe in the Gulf of Bothnia.

He had succeeded in avoiding all the trawlers and larger fish in the oceans of the world, and had now retired to the waters around the mouth of the River Ångerman, with outlying islands.

The young Baltic herring, and the sprats, looked up to him: they crowded round him in silent shoals, listening to his stories, his exhortations, and not least his warnings.

He was so incredibly ancient. Algae grew on his head; from his back, a cluster of kelp groped towards the water surface; and from his belly hung ragged sea-shells. On those few occasions when he moved, he made his way along the sea-bed with the help of a stick, held in his mouth.

"I could tell you," he said, "about Ådalen, Kramfors, Sollefteå, Örnsköldsvik, Härnösand and Junsele … but of what interest is all that to little Baltic herrings?

There are more *important* things to remember!"

There were ripples in the shoal that surrounded him, as they crowded in closer. He clearly intended to tell them something of interest.

The old herring sensed his power, savoured it, took pleasure in it. He let them all inflate with expectation.

He then prepared himself to speak.

A gang of passing perch noted that the old herring was holding court again.

The shadow of a hull slid over the sea-bed.

The old herring began his address — and at once his slow, easy manner was gone, replaced now by fire and temperament!

"Take care!" he screeched, so that some of the tiniest herring in the front row sought terrified refuge behind their larger siblings.

"Take care! Lie low!" the old herring went on. "Because they're out to make pickled herring of you! Herring pickled in mustard, pickled in tomato. And blackened 'smokies' and roll-mops!

"So take care, you daughters and sons of Poseidon!

"They're out to catch you, and salt you, and fry you, and boil you …!"

There was a great commotion in the shoal.

Some fainted, and required artificial gillification to restore them.

All trembled.

"But the worse thing of all," the ancient went on … "The worst thing of all …"

He savoured the moment.

The shoal vibrated and shook. "Out with it, then!"

"The worst thing of all," he said, "is to be made into SOUR HERRING!"

"Help!" they all cried. "Sour Herring, what's that?"

"A fate worse than death, a torment worse than wriggling in a gull's beak."

"To become Sour Herring," said the ancient "is the lowest thing that can happen to a fish. To become a sardine or an anchovy, what is that? … Sheer Paradise! But to be made into Sour Herring is humiliating. You're jam-packed into a fermenting tin, and when people finally open it they shout like savages. They gulp the juice and toss down their *brännvin*, and chew us and tear at us like ravenous sharks. Drooling, licking their chops, and protesting our excellence the while!

"This is an experience so terrifying, that no herring has ever survived it. The lack of dignity with which human beings practise this hideous ritual is so depressing, that I am ashamed on their behalf."

The old herring gave a resigned sigh. A salty tear from his fish eye was blended with the fresher water of the Bothnian.

His congregation was shaken.

And as if at a given signal the Baltic herring departed, all of them together.

They had no intention of staying in these waters any longer!

Sour Herring! Had you heard of anything so humiliating?

The old herring watched them vanish like a flash of lightning. He supported himself on his stick, and smiled. Evening had drawn in, and the light from Högbonden was playing on the surface up there.

"That's right," he thought, "off you go! Out into the salt water with you! Broaden your wavy views. Time enough for the pickling, and your Eternal Conservation."

And thus it came about that the Sour Herring Salting House in Bönhamn on the High Coast never got a single Baltic herring to ferment and keg that year.

Not even a tiddler.

by Stefan Demert

VÄSTERBOTTEN

She came walking through the forests, crossing the pathless countryside to the village where she was to work as maidservant to her father's uncle. She walked for one whole day, slept the night in a woodcutter's hut, and then walked another half day before she arrived.

At the outlying stock farms, she would stop; she was given milk and whey, and was interrogated as to who she was and where she was going. The women shook their kerchiefed heads when they heard what route she had travelled.

"Only a child," they told each other. "And all alone".

After a brief rest and discussion of her kith and kin, she set off once more with her bundle beneath her arm. In it she had a few clothes, and a catachism, a departing gift from her grandfather.

"Read it, girl," he had said. "Read and fear the Lord".

"And work!" her mother added, anxious that reading might make her idle. To toil in the sweat of your brow was the human condition, and woe betide the person who forgot it.

Her bundle also contained a stone. A remarkable stone which she had found that same morning by the hut where she had spent the night. It was smooth and white, like a chicken's egg in shape but larger than her fisted hands together. Such a stone could not be just left lying in the forest, she had somehow seen it as having lain there among the spruce and brushwood since time immemorial, to be discovered, ultimately, by precisely herself. It weighed her down heavily, but was nonetheless a comfort to have tucked under her arm.

Arriving at the pastures that separated the village, and its tilled soil, from the forests, she stopped. Down by the lake, she saw the long, narrow village: crouching grey houses, a few others painted red, and the chapel shining white. She heard the dogs barking, and the sound of human voices; the coughing of a sheep, and a child crying. The sun was casting gold into the lake, as she gently whispered the one word "Grandfather ...".

She was 13, short of stature, but self-assured enough and quick of mind. She had made the long journey by herself, and been fearful for wood-sprites and bears; but she had not turned back, and had cried only a little. Now, looking down over the village, she hesitated, afraid to go further.

The perils of the forests she knew, but here a new and unknown life was awaiting her. She stood there for a long time, but in the end she moved on. To a new life of work, first as a maidservant, later as a farmer's wife. She bore four sons, acquired numerous grandchildren, and spent her declining years in the Home – the home of her childhood, she never saw again.

The child lays its sun-baked cheek against the strangely smooth stone, so cool despite the stifling heat.

"Mummy, tell me about Old Grandma!".

And her mother tells her the story: "She came walking through the forests ...".

by Åsa Lind

NORRBOTTEN

The break-up of the ice in the River Torne
The warmth arrives on one of the earliest days in May. The still-thick cover of snow rapidly melts away. Thousands of rivulets combine to form streams, which run down into the river. The water rises.

The people living along the shores observe developments. For generations, they have been able to read the local landscape. When a hole in the ice appears over the centre of the river bed, where the current is strongest, they know that the "débacle", the breaking up of the ice, will start two days later. It's a sure sign.

The ice edges back from the river banks. Everywhere, cracks can be seen across the river, from bank to bank. A few hours later, the ice starts moving. Floes half a kilometre long release their grip, only to latch themselves fast again. The water rises rapidly. The floes break off, float loose, buffet against the land, and push trees and bushes in front of them. Ice floes tens of metres long, and still a metre or more thick, are pressed up onto the islands. New floes come loose up-river, float with the waters, and jostle along the river, crunching to pieces, sliding up on each other's backs, getting squeezed upright on their edges.

Suddenly, there is a stoppage downstream. A large ice-floe is jammed between an island and the Finnish shore. New floes come down with the current. Banks of ice, tens of metres high, are formed in mid-river, floes are pressed below the water, and clog the river down by its bed. The vast masses of descending water are unable to pass.

The ice-clot holds, and the water rises rapidly. The level is higher now than in the River's larger sister, Torne Water. The current turns.

On the road bridge over the Water, the villagers gather to see what is happening. The water is pressed between the pillars of the bridge; ice floes follow and crash into the bridge, the iron railings vibrate but the structure holds.

The water is now rising very quickly indeed. One metre. Two metres. Before nightfall, the water has risen three and a half metres, flooding over the banks. Out in the fields, the water licks the roofs of the little hay-barns.

The pressure is so enormous that the ice-clot gives way, and without warning the ice starts to move again. First further down-river; then floe after floe comes loose. Pushed by the water, the floes roll, are pressed upright on their edges, and topple over. Now that they are in motion, nothing will be able to stop the great masses of ice. They carry with them everything in their path.

It's been like this since time immemorial, long before there was any human settlement here. Some years are gentler, others like this one. But the floods don't simply cause damage. They also fertilize the ground, so that Tornedalen is the most fertile valley in Sweden.

During the spring floods of 1615, the river broke open a new path just north of Övertorneå, carrying with it Särkilax Chapel, one of the northernmost outposts of Christendom.

In the spring of 1677, one Antti Mikkelinpoika Keksi, peasant, soldier, and poet, sat on the stone outside his little cottage high up on the slopes of Torakankorva, and composed a song, 106 lines long, about the violent spring floods in the river below. Keksi was a contemporary of Stiernhielm's, the father of Swedish poetry. Here up in the wilds, far away indeed from any Swedes with pretensions to an education, Keksi created his song, which an oral tradition has handed down from generation to generation, to our own day. In all probability, Keksi could not write. Not until 1800 was his song written down by Finnish students, impelled by a romantic interest in folk poetry.

No one has recorded the life history of Antti Mikkelinpoika. We know only that his poem is in the same ancient meter as Finland's great national epic, the Kalevala:

See the flood move Simon's Island
See it slaughter Juuso's oxen
Take a paddock in Lovikka
Pass through Pajala in fury
Give a skerry, take a farmhouse
Drag the skerry o'er the meadows

See it seize a mill in Kardis
For to grind its flour in Jarhois
Where the waters yet more violent
Might more briskly spin the millstone

On it runs to Marjosaari
But I, Keksi, from my hilltop,
Look down o'er the sloping rock face,
Torkankorva's mighty stronghold.
If the Lord should send me straightly
In His mercy some fine timber
I will split it into shingles
For the pinnacles of His Temple,
And make good our leaky church roof.
by Gunnar Kieri

LAPPLAND

A railway in the north

Early in July, he stood in the drizzle at Riksgränsen station. The fog and mist were sweeping down from the mountainsides, and he could hear the glacier-water murmuring in the *jokks*. It was a bad summer in the North.

He tried to recall how many times he had visited this grim terrain, but it had been often enough and he soon lost track. After all, it had been a late night. They'd sung the old railway navvies' songs, and drunk far too many jars of "birch leaf", the distilled liquor spiced with the first "mouse's ears" that sprouted on the Arctic birches, and tasting much the way it smells on a dance-floor on Midsummer Eve.

The silence was broken by a cacophony of shrill signals, and the extra train from Narvik that he was waiting for creaked into the station. The brightly polished instruments of a couple of brass bands protruded from the wound-down train windows, and the tones of the old navvies' song from the Ore Line rang out:

"Up between the mountains in the cold and snow/We're off to build a town, boys, where the trains can go/There'll be a mighty railroad from the ore mines to the sea/So Victoria Port, boys, is the place for me".

After a short stop, the train rolled on towards the Navvies' Cemetery in Tornehamn. A festive mood prevailed in the carriages, with Norwegian Pilsener, and aquavit in tubes. ("Care for a squeeze of the hard stuff?") Most of those taking part were clad in traditional navvy gear, with heavy waistcoats, snuff kerchiefs, and slouch-hats. They were not slow to offer a beer.

At Tornehamn the train stopped, and everyone poured out. Their mood grew slightly more subdued, as they wandered in ragged procession behind the band down to the Navvies' Cemetery.

Simple white crosses stand in a grove of contorted Arctic birches. Here rest the men and women who died of the cold and tuberculosis, the victims of the many disasters.

At a cross marked "Anna, Norway, died 10/10 1901" they laid a sledge hammer, plaited of pine brushwood. Anna, known as the "Black Bear," the cook who became a legend, and had a place in every navvy's heart.

The drizzle stops, and again the old navvies' songs resound from the brass instruments. The train is waiting to carry us on, to the Hotel Lapplandia's luxurious luncheon table, and the Railway Navigators' Festival.

by Björn Arahb

Ræg'ganan rákkisvuotta
Nu gå roan'ki soakki
årro duoddar-ravdas,
nu læ bieg'ga bådnjan
mu nai ællima.
Nu gå soagi mádda
bievla vuos'tá čuov'gá,
nu åccalan váriide, lågoide ja
åruhagaide.
Dat læ mu ællin,
man mån rákkistan.

by Paulus Utsi

A Painful Love
See any twisted birch
perched by the fell's edge:
thus is my own life,
shaped by the wind.
And as the birch's trunk
cleaves to the bare ground
so yearn I for the fells,
the high plains, the dwelling places.
Such is my life,
which I love.

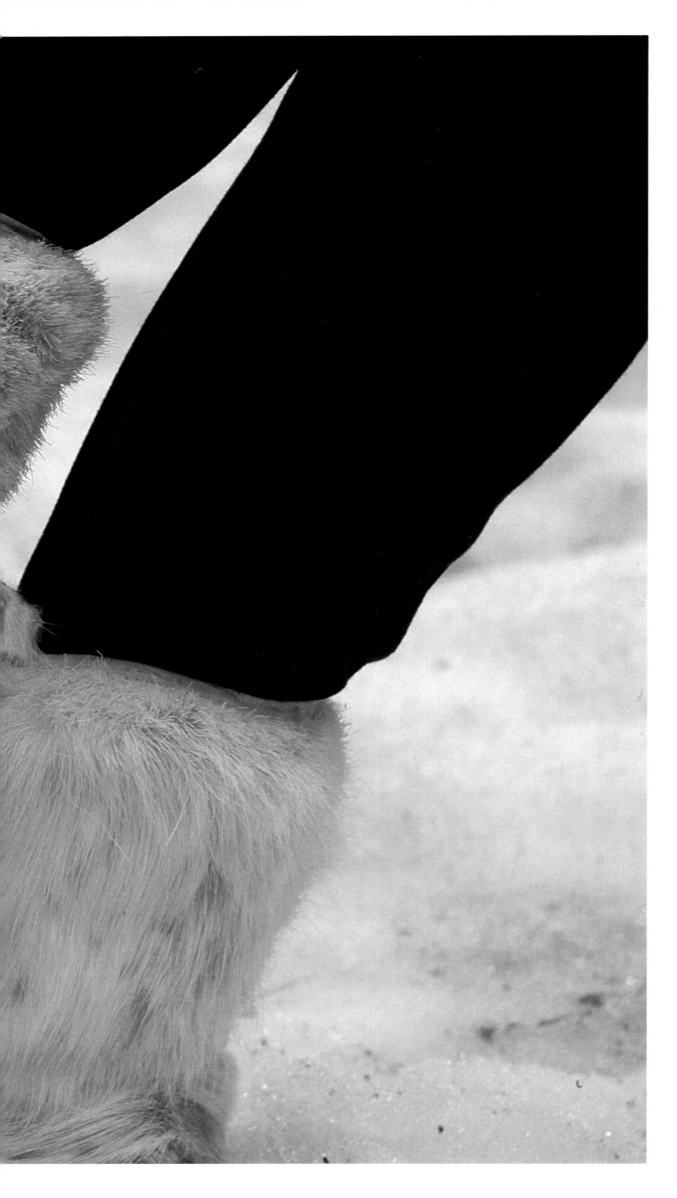

Here we come – the Lapps – the last people in this book.

But then it's usual, they say, to save the best to the last.

And this is what the State tells us, when we arrive last at the flesh pots of Swedish welfare.

We're a very peculiar people. We have no country of our own, no common language, no single church, not even a God of our own. There are only about 15,000 of us here in Sweden, and we could easily be popped away in Tensta, or some other suburb of Stockholm.

But we like to live up here in the North. We love these bare, forbidding fells. The forest product industry knows this, and supplies us amply with bare hillsides even down in the forest area.

For this, we are naturally very grateful.

We're a very peaceful people. None of our various languages contains a word for "war". History relates that we rebelled on just one occasion, and bit off the nose of a county bailiff in Kautokeino. But that was many, many years ago, and our crime must be prescribed by this time.

Everyone knows how peaceful we are. So it's easy to push us slightly to one side of the Swedish idyll, where we will cause least bother.

We are nomads, we wander far and wide. We frequently, for example, make long excursions to Rhodes, the Canary Islands and other attractive resorts. We always return, however, to the High North to sit in front of our huts, and have our photographs taken by Skanians, Smålanders, and the other strange peoples who visit us during the tourist seasons.

We are dead exotic. We dress in colourful costumes and sit making our voice music to the Midnight Sun all night – whenever the television crews arrive.

Unfortunately, we can no longer offer any real *rajd,* the bit where we set off for the hills in a mass of sleds behind our reindeer. Our Dallas cars, snow scooters, motorcycles and helicopters seem not to fit the bill.

We pursue a livelihood known as reindeer farming. This means, among other things, that some of our faithful friends are transformed into smoked reindeer steak, and served up at Nobel banquets in Stockholm. To drive in our reindeer to the pasture, for separation and slaughter, we use snow scooters and helicopters, since most of us have forgotten how to ski. Once we've got the beasts in the traps (there aren't any corrals these days), we drive over in our bus with the computers, and feed in our data on the stock.

It's all incredibly romantic.

We've stopped milking our reindeer. Not because reindeer milk turns us off, but we've found that it's far more convenient to slake our thirst with a couple of beers from the village Co-op.

Also, we no longer live in huts. Those we keep simply for the tourists to have an exotic backdrop when they take our pictures. It would look a bit daft to have us sitting there in our gear in front of our Mexi-brick houses.

We are, after all, a highly exotic and unusual people.

by Olle Rajd

INDEX OF PICTURES/PHOTOGRAPHERS

WRITERS

A brief presentation of the writers who have helped to give each province its personal touch.

BJÖRN ARAHB: Balladeer, specializing in Carl Mikael Bellman and navvies' songs. Has composed music to Ivar-Lo Johansson's "Songs from a time of schism".

STEFAN DEMERT: Writer and balladeer, creates his own music and lyrics.

NILS-PETER ECKERBOM: Author, and journalist for Nerikes Allehanda.

CHRISTER ELDERUD: Nature photographer, and journalist for Östgöta Correspondenten.

LOKA ENMARK: Author, with a bent for black humour, and a sharp eye for human frailties.

NILS FERLIN 1898–1961. Grew up in Filipstad. A central figure among Stockholm's literary bohemians during the 20s. Of all Sweden's modern poets, Ferlin is the most widely read. His poetry is characterized by a jesting sadness, a gallows humour, and reflects, often in the form of the epigram or couplet, both sharp irony, and compassion for society's unfortunates.

BO FORSBERG: Artist and author, has written a novel and three short stories. Born in Stockholm, and resident on Gotland for the past 12 years.

BO GRANDIEN: Ph. D. Assistant Professor in History of Art. Author, and on the editing staff of Dagens Nyheter.

ALF HAMBE: A poet who sings, above all others, the praises of Halland, and has created the realm of "Molom".

TOMMY HAMMARSTRÖM: Part-time farmer in Värmland, and journalist for Expressen.

ANDERZ HARNING: The scourge of Swedish bureaucracy, and an esteemed short story writer. Novelist, and columnist in Dagens Nyheter.

EINAR HECKSCHER: Poet, journalist, and translator of Anglo-Saxon literature.

TAISTO JALAMO: Journalist and film-maker. Author of "The Finns of Sweden, Then and Now".

GUNNAR KIERI: Author of e.g. the suite of novels "We're not going to make it, I'm not staying" and "Why should I lie?".

ÅSA LIND: Newly published author, makes the porridge and coffee at a small café in the Old Town, Stockholm.

OVE MAGNUSSON: Dramatist, author and journalist. Writes a great deal for radio and television.

HARRY MARTINSON: 1904–1978. Author, and from 1949 a Member of the Swedish Academy. Nobel Laureate 1974. His extensive work is dominated by the theme of liberty and vagabondage, as in his novel "The Road" (1948). He also wrote radio plays, and the space epic "Aniara" (1956).

PETER MOSSKIN: Novelist and all-round writer.

PAUL NILSSON: 1866–1951. A priest from Västgöta, with a rich literary vein. He wrote poems, hymns, sermons, lectures etc. Was honoured by an award from the Swedish Academy.

OLLE RAJD (Andersson): Journalist and editor of the magazine Samefolket ("The Lapp People").

BERNT STAF: Balladeer and poet, composer and former phytochemist. Has effectively drawn Sweden's attention to the unusual character and beauty of Österlen.

RAGNAR STRÖMBERG: West Coast poet, writer of occasional prose. Has worked a great deal with radio and television.

STIG TJERNQUIST: Art Director and copywriter with his own advertising agency in the Old Town, Stockholm.

PAULUS UTSI: 1918–1975. The great poet of the Swedish Lapps, who before he became a writer farmed reindeer and did handicraft work. His best-known collection of poetry is "Giela gielain" ("Capturing Words").

LARS WESTMAN: Editor for the cooperative magazine VI. Has written a number of books about the archipelago.

FINN ZETTERHOLM: Writer and singer. Has produced 10 or so LPs. Debates matters cultural in the daily press, and as a guest on radio and television programmes, in which the tones of his folk songs are often blended with sharp satire.

SANDRO-KEY ÅBERG: An important Swedish poet, with a past in student theatre and popular education. His unusual and powerful poetry is characterized by an expressive realism, playful observations of nature, and a direct, confidential tone.

BRITT ÅGREN: Journalist for Dagens Nyheter. Has worked for many years with the DN supplement "On the town", with fascinating and affectionate descriptions of people and places in Stockholm.

PROVINCES